TERRY DAVIES

WALES'S FIRST SUPERSTAR FULLBACK

*Dedicated to my wife and soulmate, Gillian,
my children and grandchildren, and in memory of
my brother Len who I miss to this day*

TERRY DAVIES

WALES'S FIRST SUPERSTAR FULLBACK

TERRY DAVIES
WITH GERAINT THOMAS

y Lolfa

ISBN: 978 1 78461 274 0

Published and printed in Wales
on paper from well-maintained forests by
Y Lolfa Cyf., Talybont, Ceredigion SY24 5HE
website www.ylolfa.com
e-mail ylolfa@ylolfa.com
tel 01970 832 304
fax 832 782

Contents

Foreword by Sir Gareth Edwards

ONE OF MY friends growing up in Gwaun Cae Gurwen, at the top of the Swansea Valley, was a boy called Huw Llywelyn Davies, who went on to follow in his father's footsteps and become a very respected rugby broadcaster. At that time Eic Davies did the radio reports on matches and quite often we would go along with him to grounds such as St Helen's, The Gnoll and Stradey Park to watch our heroes of the day. We all had heroes as children. I wasn't a scrum-half as such at that age, far from it, I just played rugby, and you would follow all your heroes; if Cyril Davies has a good game you wanted to be a centre or, Dewi Bebb, you wanted to be a wing or Terry Davies, a fullback.

As kids at the end of games you had a wonderful opportunity, especially down Stradey Park, to run onto the field and try to get an autograph. I can remember, vividly, getting Terry's; it was a wonderful experience as he was someone who stood out for me from a lot of exceptional players who were around at that time.

I can remember him playing clearly; to actually see a player I had read about on the back pages and seen glimpses of on the Pathé newsreel in the cinema, as there was no television back then, was so exciting.

Terry was a great positional player who was so neat, comfortable and secure under the high ball, not to mention a wonderful goal kicker who had a huge punt on him as well. He was slight by today's standards but he was defensively very strong in the tackle. As a young inspiring player he left a huge impression on me due to the way he stood out from the rest; he was such a majestic player and so meticulous in his play.

Although I can't say I recall him beating five defenders to score in the corner, he could be an attacking force when called upon and as a player he was a giant. The expectation of a fullback in those days was one of stability, and he gave his team and his supporters' strength in defence. He stood there like a rock.

Outside-halves used to get the ball and kick it high in the air so their marauding forwards could chase it up and attempt to dismember the waiting fullback, but Terry was always cool, calm and collected, not to mention brave under the high ball. And then he would be deadly accurate with his return kicking. He exuded confidence to the rest of the team.

I also saw him play for Wales in that epic game against South Africa in Cardiff when it rained all day. I had been given a brand-new duffle coat by my mother and I remember that even though we were in the north enclosure under the north stand watching, it was still so wet that when I went to pull the hood over my head it was half-full of water. There was that much rain falling! Terry just failed with a huge kick; how he managed to get it out of that mud at all I will never know.

Another kick of his that sticks in the mind was when he hit the crossbar from practically his own half against a gale-force wind at Twickenham. Someone later cut the crossbar down. I remember following the story with great delight at the time and I remember the wonderful gesture, as he was a timber merchant, of offering to replace it!

Following the 1959 British and Irish Lions tour, Terry is revered in New Zealand as one of the great players of that era – even though they had their own star fullback in Don Clarke who was kicking the penalties while the Lions were scoring the tries – he was outstanding in a side that was very unlucky to lose the series. To be nominated one of the players of the series, as was Terry, was some feat, there's no doubt about it.

Finally, the question that is often posed when it comes to former players: would Terry Davies play for Wales today? Absolutely. As with all great players he had the athleticism and the rugby brain to play at the highest level in any generation.

John yr Ynys

IT IS WRITTEN in the folklore of west Wales that in the early 1860s a farm labourer from the wilds of Rhandirmwyn, near the market town of Llandovery, arrived in Llanelli looking for work.

He took over the running of Ynys Farm on the outskirts of the town where the giant Trostre tinplate works stands today, and married a local girl with whom he fathered nine children.

John yr Ynys, as he became known, also had a passion for religion and became a lay preacher of note, regularly attracting congregations of up to 2,000 souls.

A local myth testifies that in the late 1890s the area was hit by a great drought and farm animals were dying everywhere. Around eight weeks into the crisis, John yr Ynys got onto his knees, when the moon was shining, and prayed to the Good Lord to bring rain. The next morning, his hitherto dried-up well was full of water and people came from far and wide with their animals to be saved.

The 'miracle' of John yr Ynys saw him become known across the land and his life was chronicled in a Welsh-language book at the turn of the last century.

However, for followers of Welsh rugby, who take time to study his genealogy, the real miracle of John yr Ynys is that he provided an almost unrivalled seam of talent to the national side.

The first of his line to play for Wales was lock Samuel Gethin Thomas, from Llwynhendy, who was capped in 1923 playing all four games of that season's Five Nations Championships. Next came his great-grandsons, the talented Bynea brothers, Terry and Len Davies, to cement the legacy. The world then held its breath as the regal Barry John raised the bar to new

John yr Ynys

heights while his brother, Alan, toured Argentina with Wales and another brother, Clive, was capped at B level. The little magician that was Jonathan Davies carried on the tradition before the trio of Scott, Craig and Gavin blessed the union of Barry John's sister, Madora, and one Derek Quinnell.

As Terry Davies proclaims, 'If the Welsh Rugby Union had been able to freeze John yr Ynys's sperm, my God, what a team we could have had in Wales!'

This is the Terry Davies story.

CHAPTER 1

Stunned during Grenade Training

(Dartmoor, Tuesday, 13 January 1953)

I HEAR THAT these days Welsh players are informed of team selection by text message, such is the wonder of modern technology. Even if mobile phones had been invented in my day I doubt very much whether there would have been a signal on the wild and windy mountain top I found myself on shortly after the team to face England, in the opening fixture of the 1953 Five Nations Tournament, had been finalised.

I had been delighted to have been asked to play in the final Welsh trial in Cardiff that year – back then there were three trials for the national side, all of which were fiercely contested – and shortly afterwards, being in the Royal Marines at the time, I headed back to my base in Plymouth.

To be honest with you I didn't think that I had much chance of being selected, as the incumbent fullback, Llanelli's Gerwyn Williams, was an excellent player who had never let his country down. I was just happy to have caught the eye of the selectors at the tender age of 19 with little more than two seasons in senior rugby under my belt, and so set my sights on settling back into military life. I was literally brought back down to earth with a bang as the next day I found myself on one of the highest points of Dartmoor for a spot of grenade training.

It was a miserable, freezing cold day with a little bit of snow on the ground. There were eight of us sat in a circle busily inserting detonators into the grenades; we were well-spaced out in case someone made a mistake and one went off! You were then called forward, one at a time, to join the sergeant in a trench. He would say to you, 'Now this grenade has a seven-second fuse, so after you pull the pin out and throw it, I don't want you to take cover straightaway, I want you to look where it lands.' None of us ever looked. As soon and it left your hand you dived to the floor!

In between the explosions we heard the sound of a jeep making its way up from the valley below. When it arrived, and pulled to an abrupt stop, a sergeant jumped out and asked our sergeant rather gruffly, 'Have you got a Private Davies here?'

When he was given an affirmative answer he barked, 'Well the Commanding Officer wants to see him immediately!'

I thought, 'Good God. I must have done something wrong. I'm in trouble.'

I was called forward and ordered into the jeep and it shot off back down the valley towards our base in Bickleigh. On the journey I plucked up the courage to ask the sergeant what it was all about and he replied, 'All I know is that you're in front of the CO. It must be serious whatever it is.'

When we arrived at the barracks I was given five minutes to change into my best Blues; that's when I really began to worry.

Once changed, I was marched across the compound to the CO's office and told to wait in a room just outside. All of a sudden this sergeant screeched, 'Quick march! Left, right, left, right!' and in I went.

The CO, Lieutenant Colonel Madoc, stood up behind his desk and reached his hand out to shake mine. It was only then that a flashbulb went off inside my head and he said, 'Congratulations Davies, you've been selected to play for Wales.'

Well I didn't know what to say, I was over the moon. I had

light feet and a light head. I left that office floating on air and I thought, 'Bloody marvellous. I've been picked for Wales!' It was the greatest feeling in the world but there was one problem – there I was in a British army camp in the south-west of England with not a Welshman in sight to share my news with!

I looked at the sergeant who had escorted me there and he just growled, 'Right you. You've got ten minutes to change back into your combats and I'll take you back.'

When I arrived back at the compound I got out of the jeep and reported to my regular sergeant, who being Scottish, was a fellow Celt.

He asked, 'What's up then Davies? What did the CO want with you?'

'He told me that I've been selected to play for my country against England in rugby,' I replied still a bit shocked.

'Congratulations,' the sergeant said before asking, 'How much time have you got off?'

'Two days,' I said.

'Och, if you were English you would have had a week off!' he said.

CHAPTER 2

Bynea in the Blood

I AM IN danger of running ahead of myself here, so to take some advice from the pen of the great Dylan Thomas, let's begin at the beginning.

My story started in the Carmarthenshire village of Bynea – just on the right side of the River Loughor for all Scarlets supporters – and being part of the fourth generation of my family to build a life there, I have never wanted to belong anywhere else.

I was born on 24 September 1932, a date not without significance in the Davies family history. My grandfather was also born on 24 September, as was my sister, Marina, two years after me and, a few decades later, my youngest son, Matthew, arrived in this world on the same date. Now that may strike you as being quite coincidental – but when you stop and think about it, you could surmise that the couples in my family really liked to enjoy themselves at Christmas time!

It could also be just a case of the law of averages, certainly in my instance, as I was one of six children; three boys, myself and older brothers Roy and Len, later followed by three girls, Yvonne, Denise and Marina. We lived in a row of old miners' homes in Cwmfelin Road in what could be described as a typical working-class household. It was coal fires, oil lamps and when we went to bed I shared a room with my brothers. I can remember the scurrying of mice in the attic keeping me awake until my father, Ted, would tap the ceiling and there would be quiet. Then, when we got up in the morning, there would be black beetles scurrying across the bare floorboards.

Bath time for us boys was on a Friday night in front of the kitchen fire. The tin bath, hung on the outside of the house, would be brought in, while a few large kettles would boil up the water above the fire. It was quite an event and my mother, Vera, had a real production line going with us being bathed in sequence from oldest to youngest. I would be third and it was great to be washed in front of the fire while our pants, vests and socks would be in the little oven, next to the hearth, to warm before we went to bed.

Once we had all been bathed it would be my father's turn. The bath was a bit small for him but he got in nonetheless and my mother would scrub his back. Now there were three spinsters, Maggie, Gerty and Gwyneth, living next door and it seemed as though every time my father got into the bath one of them would be knocking at the door asking to borrow some sugar or milk. They would come into the kitchen and my father would be furious. He would throw the washing cloth at them shouting 'Get out!', in Welsh of course, as that was our first language.

There was no inside lavatory so, like almost every other house in the village, we had a toilet at the bottom of the garden. We used to have great fun as boys catching the largest spiders we could find and making our way to wherever the girls in the village lived. We would pop them into their toilets and then hide until these girls appeared, to answer the call of nature. Of course there would be great hilarity when the girls would run out screaming with their knickers hanging down below their knees.

On the subject of toilets there was a cesspit cart, otherwise known as the shit cart, which used to pass through the village every Monday morning. The business was run by two brothers, Jim and John Griffiths, and they would empty the cesspits of the posh people in the village; the less well-off used to bury their waste in the garden. Now we knew it was on its rounds because of the smell and, as the cart approached, you would hear all the windows and doors being slammed shut. As the cart passed through it would be followed by a regiment of flies and, woe betide any old collier with a bad chest caught in its path, as he would be left leaning against a wall coughing his guts out in its wake.

The cart would make its way to a small river behind our row of houses, called Yr Afon Goch (The Red River), and its contents would be tipped in the water to be washed out to the main estuary. The story goes that one day Jim had put his coat on the back of the cart and when it was tipped the wind blew the garment in with the effluent.

Jim said, 'I've got to get the coat!'

He took his shoes off and started rolling his trousers up when his brother said, 'Just leave the coat Jim, it's only an old thing!'

To which Jim replied, 'What do you mean? My sandwiches are in the pocket.'

One of my earliest recollections is of going to school when I was three years old. I vaguely remember oak flooring, half-glass doors, coal fires and my first teacher, Mrs Bowser, who I recollect because every time she made me sing in class she would give me a present – such as two slices of ham – to go home with. I was her favourite really.

I was quite a star in our village school and it wasn't because of any early sporting prowess but because of my sweaters. As with most large families back then, my clothes were hand-me-downs. My eldest brother Roy had them first, then they were passed on to Len, and, unfortunately, by the time they arrived with me they were well worn. However, my mother was a whiz with a needle and she was able to recycle various pieces of wool to reknit the sweater in different colours. Joseph and his Technicolor Dream Coat had nothing on me.

The school had around 400 children from a probable village population of 1,200, which is an indication that contraception had not arrived in Bynea by that time! Sadly, neither had the level of medical care that we enjoy today. I distinctly remember that we had quite a number of sick children with disabilities amongst us; it was just how life was.

When mothers heard that the next door neighbour's children had measles, mumps or the like, they would send their own children to play with them so that they would catch it and get it over with. I remember us three brothers had the measles together, and being stuck in a semi-dark room for about a week, full of blisters. And then you had the dreadful cough, the croup they used to call it. It went on for weeks and weeks; you couldn't get rid of it. Then someone had the bright idea that if you breathed steam into your lungs it would clear. So consequently you would see Llanelli station full of mothers with their children, taking the train up to Swansea. When you got to Cockett tunnel all these kids would have their heads stuck out of the window to breath in the air. Then you saw an extraordinary sight of kids with black spots all over their faces before later grimacing as their mothers spit-washed them clean again. I had my head squeezed out of the train window but I wasn't much better after it.

My mother was a great cook and we were never short of food. How she managed with six children and a husband to feed, I don't really know; it must have been very difficult. We regularly had rabbit or *cawl*, the thick Welsh stew, and on Saturdays my mother always cooked egg, bacon, cockles and laverbread for lunch; I miss them to this today. Sunday dinner was always a treat as we would have one of the chickens we kept in the back garden. My father, however, would always ruin the meal when he'd say, 'Damn, Daisy tastes really good!'

Later we moved to an end house in Bevan's Road which had a small side window with a deep windowsill, where my mother used to allow her delicious cooking to cool. On one occasion she had made an apple tart. The smell was so wonderful that my brothers and I decided that we simply had to taste it. When my mother noticed that there was a large slice missing, she was furious and sat us down.

'Now, I want you to tell me which one of you took the tart.' There was a deathly silence. No-one was going to tell on anybody and this went on for a while.

Then my mother said, 'God has seen whoever took that piece of tart. He is everywhere and sees everything, so own up now.'

My brother Len piped up, 'Are you sure that God sees everything?'

'Yes,' she said.

Then Len said, 'Perhaps it was God that took it?'

Despite the hardship, although we didn't see it as such as kids, there were many in the village far worse off than ourselves. In the 1930s there was a shortage of accommodation, especially for the poorer people. Some solved this problem through buying disused railway carriages and siting them in the old Genwen Quarry. Now there must have been about seven or eight of these homes, with little stone chimneys and the inside converted into a bedroom, kitchen and living area. They were quite comfortable really, with old windows which had the leather straps with holes to open and close them.

Some of the characters living in the carriages were very quaint people indeed. There was Billy Twlpin – he couldn't have been very poor though because he kept some pigs in a walled area at the back. Billy must have been a very good eater because he was the fattest man in Bynea. Whenever you passed through he would be sitting on the pigsty wall with his tummy hanging out; all the kids used to call him Humpty Dumpty. Then there was Harry Cooper, who was unusual because he was the spitting image of Charlie Chaplin. He was a very thin little boy, who always had his hands in his pockets, with his feet sticking out at odd angles; he was known as Harry Cooper Quarter To Three.

The village was full of characters, not least a married

woman called Rachel who was even bigger than Billy Twlpin. She lived in Cwmfelin Row with her collier husband Dan. They used to be woken in the morning by the tapper, employed by the local colliery to tap each collier's window with his stick at 5.30am so that everybody would arrive in work by 6am. One morning Dan had overslept and woke in a panic. He said to his wife, 'What do you think the time is?'

She replied, 'I'll dress quick and go outside to ask someone.'

She threw on some flimsy garments and rushed out of the door in time to see the station master passing on his bicycle. She shouted out, 'Station Master, please have you got the time?'

He looked at her flimsily dressed, and said, 'Well, I haven't got time at this particular moment but I could call back.'

Another real character was a gentleman known as Danny the Red. His family had always been very left wing and he was seen as a bit of a communist. He liked to stir it up in the pubs; within ten minutes of him entering there would be chaos. He had this knack of riling everybody. On one occasion somebody berated him for not being a good citizen. Now he had served his time in the Welsh Guards and said, 'I fought for my King and I was shot in Dunkirk!'

He rolled his sleeve up and there were scars where a bullet had gone through the back of his arm and exited the front. Suddenly a little voice came from the back, 'So, you were running away were you?'

It was a different world back then. When I was around seven years old, John Rees, of Gwtenmal Farm, bought the village's first motor car; it was a Morris 6, and everyone was full of excitement. Now you didn't need a driving licence in those days which was not necessary a good thing. Come the Sunday morning the old farmer decided to take his family for a run across the Loughor Bridge and back. The car appeared to run on a type of kangaroo petrol. A gate had been opened to let the car out of the farm but some well-intentioned neighbour had since closed it. On his return, and seeing the way blocked, the old farmer panicked and, thinking he was still on his horse and cart, instead of breaking he shouted, 'Whoa! Whoa!' before smashing into the gate and taking his vehicle's big headlamps clean off.

To keep us occupied during the school holidays, my mother would give us a pencil and paper each and sit us out front, on the pavement, telling us to record the number plates of everything that passed. We'd be there all morning and only see the baker's van and two trolley buses. It's difficult to imagine when you see the number of cars on the road today.

There was an archway in the middle of the terrace on Cwmfelin Road which gave access to the back of the houses. On wash days, you would be greeted by the sight of a hundred yards of washing dancing on the breeze. I used to go through that arch and stand amongst all the bed sheets flapping in the wind. They would make a terrific noise and I would close my eyes and think, 'I'm on the deck of Francis Drake's ship and off to attack the Spanish Armada!'

You could also identify who was living in which house by the array of underwear on display. You had nappies, pants, knickers and long johns (for the older generation), and of course, there was no mistaking where Rachel lived as she used to wear red bloomers and they were like wind socks! They were the biggest things I'd ever seen in my life.

The winters were very hard in those days; really cold but you sort of got used to it. I remember skating on ponds around the village – even skating by moonlight – when all the boys used to take a run-up from the grass onto the pond; you could glide for 20 or 30 yards if you didn't fall over.

In the summer we'd all go down to what was termed the marsh, which was the section of the estuary closest to the village, and when the tide was out we would either catch flatfish or cross over to Penclawdd to pick cockles. We had to be careful of the turning of the tide because there would be a long walk home if we missed it.

We also used to scramble on the old Bynea tip where all the village boys would meet to play Cowboys and Indians or other games.

When it came to sport we lived right opposite Bynea Welfare Park, which, you could say, was my first arena. I have been fortunate to play in stadia around the world with various teams but I suppose you can trace it all back to those countless hours spent running around that field. It would never happen today, but at that time you would see a group of 50 children playing until it became too dark to remain outside.

What a difference a generation makes. We had such wonderful times as kids running wild in the fresh air, and now all the children have computers and are stuck in the house most of the time.

We played everything from rugby to football or tennis to cricket, depending on the season and the mood. It wasn't the best of fields but, having been paid for by the community itself, it was ours.

If we had a rugby ball we would pick two teams and swarm about like bees chasing a pot of honey. It would be 20-something-a-side and, as the pitch was quite narrow, it was a real challenge to evade tackles with such little space on offer. Those games really helped develop the craft of stepping and dodging. Invariably such games always resulted in the loss of buttons and ripped shirts and there were more than a few rows when boys went home after it grew too dark to play.

When it came to cricket, the wicket was a bit tufted up so when you faced a fast bowler, you never knew where the ball would go. Despite this, we had some cracking games there. On one occasion it was a tight finish and we had drawn a bit of a crowd. As the game neared its conclusion, one of the boys hit a six. The ball soared in the air with all eyes on it when suddenly this gentleman, by the name of John Wheeler, walked onto the field, looked up, and said, 'Right boys, leave it to me!'

He put his hands up and missed the ball entirely. The ball hit him on the head and flattened him. He was lying on the ground with a big lump visibly rising on his forehead. I remember someone saying in Welsh, 'He's got one of those swellings, like they put in comics, appearing on his forehead'.

It's funny how nicknames derive and after that he went through life known as John gad e i fi (John leave it to me).

I was a quiet boy, blond haired and blue eyed, but I was a real rascal at times and would scale anything that was climbable in the village. You will learn later about the injuries I suffered through rugby but as a kid I broke bones for fun. I had broken my leg before the age of seven and more was to follow when, one Sunday morning, a racing pigeon was blown off course from somewhere or other and landed in our garden.

The little chap appeared quite tame so we tried to catch him. He managed to escape our clutches, fly across the road and settle on the front of Beria Chapel. Being the best climber, I proceeded to climb up onto the window (as the congregation was singing away merrily inside), and then, three quarters of the way up on the little roof over the entrance, I lost my footing and fell 20 feet or so, landing with a clatter, on the steps below. I was knocked out and when I came around there was a man in a brown Sunday best suit, with a big moustache on his face, looking down at me.

I looked up at him and he said, 'Oh, not this little bugger again!'

My arm was broken in two places and my wrist hung down at an odd angle.

I managed to get up and my brothers took me home. After much chastising, my father walked me up to Llwynhendy to see Doctor Hughes. When we arrived we were told that the doctor was out but his wife, who had been a nurse, offered to try and set my arm.

'I'll do my best but you'll have to take him to hospital in the morning,' she said.

She twisted and straightened my arm and my wrist before turning to my father and asking, 'Is there something wrong with him?'

'No,' my father said not understanding, 'he's just a very busy boy.'

'Well that's strange,' she replied, 'he hasn't cried once.'

The next morning I had to walk to Llanelli hospital with my father – we didn't have money to pay for the bus – and I was put in plaster of Paris for six weeks.

The doctor told my father, 'This boy is keeping me in a job!'

We didn't have large supermarkets or out of town retail parks back then but our village was alive with shops of all kind. There was Edwards' Shop, which, with its wooden interior that hadn't changed for a century or more, sold everything you could want; the Post Office and Lewis' paper shop, alongside Jack Thomas the butcher. You knew Christmas had arrived when a pig with an orange in its mouth appeared in the window of the butcher's; all the kids in the village would gather to stare through that window because we didn't see many oranges in those days.

As kids we naturally all loved Mrs Gunn's sweet shop and then you had Thomas Daniel, who was selling a little bit of petrol and sweets, and then there was Willy Griffiths the Top Shop who would sell fruit. At the very end of the village was the billiard hall, which as far as my mother was concerned, was a den of iniquity. She used to warn us. 'If you ever look inside that place God will strike you down!' Each time we passed by we would cross to the other side of the road.

One of the most useful shops was Fred Griffiths' Bake House which, for a small charge, allowed the villagers to make use of its large oven to cook their bread or meat, especially at Christmas time. The smell from the bake house used to permeate through the village with its hot freshly cooked loaves, and still lingers in my nostrils today; it was marvellous. Fred's even had its own resident ghost which appeared about 7 o'clock each morning to walk down the street. That white spherical figure was, of course, the baker finishing his shift covered in flour!

At the top end of the village was the cobbler, Griff y Crydd, who would repair your shoes. Footwear would last you years because they would be re-soled over and over again. I remember going there as a boy and waiting for my shoes to be repaired. Talking to Griff would be quite an experience as he would have all these tacks hanging out of his mouth; he'd take them out one at a time and nail them in talking all the while.

Years later, before setting off to make my debut for Wales, I took my boots up to Griff to have the studs changed. He did a magnificent job and when it came to paying he gave them back to me free of charge with all his best wishes. I shall always remember him for that but I'm sure it was the first time he ever did a job for free!

Although surrounded by estuary and fields, Bynea has a rich industrial past that has shaped the village, its landscape and people. The estuary itself has a huge history and was once an important Roman port, accessing a large fort at Loughor. When I cross the bridge, and the sun is shining, I look across the water and I can imagine a fleet of Roman warships filling up the estuary.

At one time there were three major pits in the village, the Genwen, Glynea and Pencoed, which employed around a thousand miners during the early 1900s but they had all closed by the time I came along. It was said that the pits thrived in the village during the First World War because they produced the best steam coal in the country. The Royal Navy couldn't get enough of it; they said it gave their ships two knots of extra speed over the German fleet! It is also rumoured that Bynea coal was firing the furnaces of the *Titanic* when it sank.

There were also brick, steel and tinplate works in the village, all shaping the way we lived, through employment and the way the work moulded those who carried it out; men were hard as nails in those days and made for playing rugby!

My grandfather, Jonah Morris, who had played rugby for Bynea, was a great historian. He taught me to respect and value our heritage through his countless stories. He had worked in the Genwen and told me that one of its seams ran just 40 metres below the surface. When it did a little hiccup, and travelled upwards, they were digging so close to the village floor that they could hear the milkman bringing his cart around in the mornings.

Grimly, it was also the scene of a disaster that shook the village when a fire broke out underground leaving five men dead. Unfortunately, in the immediate aftermath, nobody would go down to attempt a rescue, as there were fears of further explosions. Then the son of one of the trapped miners, he was only 18 years old, appeared and was determined to try and save his father so he went in the cage. He too was lost. The pit never reopened.

Sadly, the other two pits remained closed following the General Strikes of 1926; they became flooded and their owners just didn't bother with the expense of getting them work-ready again.

Life underground was tough but there were also lighter moments as my grandfather would recall. One of the pubs in the village used to run a pot of money, which the miners paid into, and at the end of the year it would go to the man who had accomplished the biggest feat over that period. On one occasion the pot had got to around ten guineas. Soon after, this collier was digging away on the lower seam in the Glynea pit when the roof came down. He was covered with debris and his friends rushed in to drag him out. They pronounced him dead in the grim darkness of the mine, gently transferred him to a stretcher and covered him with a blanket.

All the hooters went off, signalling a disaster, and within minutes everyone in the village came out to line the streets. They brought this gentleman to the surface and carried him home, through the streets where the women were all out crying. His wife stood outside his gate, full of tears, to meet him. Then, suddenly, the blanket was whipped to one side and up he got.

He turned to the stretcher bearers and said, 'Thanks for the lift home boys. I think this trick should win the pot!'

My father worked in the St David's Tinworks and was part of a team of four. To see those men working in unison was really magnificent; any mistake could have chopped off somebody's leg. The way that the tinplate slid across the floor, to be grabbed by their tongs, and then shifted onto the next one, and then through the mill before being lifted and humped into the furnace again, was quite something.

In the hot summers my mother would give me two large pop bottles to take down to the works for my dad. I'd walk all the way down and listen to the work's huge fly-wheel; it was a superb sound because it ran so quietly and yet it whistled. It was like a magnet to see it. My father would sink the two bottles of pop inside a minute; there would be white crystal crust all over his face where he was losing salt, so you had to put some liquids back in. He wore a flannel around his neck to absorb the moisture and I'll always remember him taking his clogs off and emptying the sweat out of them.

While on the subject of my father, it is fair to say I benefited from his sporting genes. He was an excellent all-round sportsman. He could swim the Loughor River between the railway bridge and the old road bridge, from one side to the other and back again, with the tide coming in at a hell of a rate. He was also a good athlete and played soccer for Llanelli and for Lovells, which was quite a good side in those days, and at one stage a scout came down from Middlesbrough to offer him a trial, but he was a bit of a home bird so turned them down. As a footnote, his own father, Rees Davies, was a good rugby player as well, by all accounts, having played for Bridgend in the 1900s.

Life in the village was to change drastically in 1939 when the Second World War broke out. We were issued gas masks and the school windows had strips of glued paper placed on them in little squares so, if bombed, the glass would only splinter in small amounts. Being children it was rather an exciting time because each time the air-raid siren sounded we had to leave school and run to a specified house for shelter. My mother was perturbed by this and insisted that her three children stay together because she couldn't bear to lose one of us; she would rather lose us all than just one!

It became a waiting game. We would go to school in the hope that the air-raid siren would sound so we could rush out to the home of Hetty Rees, where we had a place to sit under the table. We watched and waited all day long for the siren to go because every time we went to Hetty's house her mother would have sandwiches, cakes and cups of tea waiting under that table!

When the bombing of Swansea started a year or so later it became quite a frightening time for young and old alike. My father would put me up on his shoulders, take me through the garden and on to the Genwen tip at the back of the house. It was the highest point of the village and all the men used to gather there and watch Swansea burning. You could see the sky lit up with terrific flames as the bombs landed. It is something that will stay with me for the rest of my life. We would sometimes travel into Swansea just to have a look at the destruction. As we approached the town there would be all these barrage balloons, flapping about 300 feet in the air, to stop the low flying planes coming in.

A blackout was introduced and you couldn't see further

than your nose when you got out of the house. If you showed any light in the village you would land a one-guinea fine, which was about a week's wages. Now our air-raid warden, Edgar Titus Hopkins, was the vicar's son but he had no charity to him whatsoever. You can imagine the large number of children in the village unable to resist the temptation of peeping through those curtains; virtually half the village had been fined by that dreadful man. Revenge did take place, however. Apart from his cruel nature, he was known for having a glorious apple tree, the fruit of which would win him the top award in the local fêtes or shows. He was always very smug about it but the smile was wiped off his face when, on VE Day, somebody took an axe to his beloved tree!

In the summer we would play outside until 11 o'clock when the darkness would come along with the German planes on their way to bomb Swansea. Sometimes they used to mistake the estuary for Swansea Bay, or perhaps the pilots were frightened and just dropped their bombs anywhere and left, but we seemed to be in the centre of a rain of incendiary bombs. You would hear the thundering of the planes overhead and the screeching of these bombs coming down. The next day you would go for a walk to find huge amounts of these bombs stuck in the marsh area of the village.

When the air-raid warning sounded outside of school hours we would go next door to the three spinsters and hide under their table. They were as much afraid as us children. Now they ran the village chip shop and the best part of it all was after the air raid, when they would put the chip pan on and we would have a few chips before going back to bed. We were later told that gathering under the table was not a good idea, so room was made under the stairs. We would all crouch there in great fear. You would hear some very large bombs dropping in the area and the old house used to shake. Maggie would say to Gerty, 'Have you got the bag?' And she would have to run upstairs to get this leather satchel which apparently had all the money from the selling of chips; she would sit there cwtching that bag while all these bombs were coming down.

At that time the old Pencoed tin works, which had become a scrapyard, was taken over by the RAF as a kind of graveyard for its planes. They used to bring all these broken planes in on these 60-foot trailers: Spitfires, Hurricanes, you name it, they ended up in Bynea to be broken up and recycled. Being kids we used to sneak under the wire and sit in the cockpits and play out imaginary dog fights. What a playground it was until we found somebody's finger on a cockpit's floor!

The war years and the RAF were also memorable for another event in my life... watching my first game of rugby. In 1940 a team was raised from what Bynea men were still available, following conscription, to play against a side from a small RAF base near the village.

It was a nice sunny afternoon and most of the village turned out at the old Glynea Farm ground to watch. The home side had managed to acquire the service of a ringer in the form of a gentleman called Dan Griffiths, who had played a couple of games for London Welsh. I remember him well because he was a very stylish man; the first ever person that I saw wearing plus-four trousers; all us kids were agog at this very splendid figure.

He was a powerful man and took his position on the wing. When the ball came to him he started snorting through his nose and set off like a bull. He bludgeoned everyone out of his way, along the touchline, until he was met by several covering players on the corner flag, who shoulder-barged him into touch. Now a few feet away was a wooden garage and suddenly Dan Griffiths, unable to stop, simply disappeared into this wooden garage, leaving a big hole in the back of it. For years after, anytime we went down to watch a game, you would see a patched up section in what had become known as Dando's garage!

CHAPTER 3

A Rugby Education at Stradey School

SEPTEMBER 1942 SAW me leave Bynea's village school behind and head off to Stradey Central School in Llanelli. I will never forget my first day in secondary school. I was out of my comfort zone, standing amongst all these strange new kids, but it was the same for everyone and I soon settled in. It was a large school but a very good school, well managed by the headmaster, Brinley Evans, of whom we were all in awe because, as a tough hooker, he had played rugby for Wales.

They were happy days and I was given the honour of being a milk monitor, tasked with taking the crates around the different classrooms. It was quite a perk, as you were allowed out of lessons. I wasn't that interested in education; I enjoyed history and Welsh, but maths was like a foreign language to me and English was not easy being from such a Welsh-speaking background. Luckily, the teachers didn't seem too bothered in forcing you to do well in your studies as there was plenty of work in the steelworks or the mines.

We were still touched by the war and when the air-raid siren sounded we would all have to run into Stradey Woods, which was adjacent to the school, and hide until the all clear. In the autumn we used to make the most of the opportunity to pick chestnuts which we would later roast. Those woods, which belonged to the Mansel Lewis family who lived in Stradey Castle, were usually out of bounds but sometimes we would sneak into them at lunchtimes to collect extra chestnuts. On one occasion I was caught along with two of my friends and we faced being caned by Mr Evans in assembly the following morning. When the time came for our punishment, one of our trio, John y Beili, a farmer's son, didn't appear.

Now when you were caned you tried your best to look chastised and you would never meet the teacher's eyes because if he thought you were defying him you would get it even harder. The poor lad with me kept taking his hand away so in the end he was really hammered.

When we went back to the classroom, who should be sitting there, all smiles, but John y Beili. I said to him, 'Why weren't you caned with us?' To which he replied, 'Ah, my father came down with half a dozen eggs for the headmaster.' Eggs were a rarity during the war I can tell you.

Rationing had really hit us hard but there was always ways to get extra food, including keeping livestock. You knew a pig was being killed in the village because you would hear screams in the morning; everybody was waiting with bated breath for it to stop. We kids would hang around the house wherever the pig was being killed and wait for the bladder to be given to us so we could play soccer with it; after ten minutes or so it always got fractured.

Now the village bobby would walk the village every day but the day the pig was killed he had a day off. The next day he would call in the house and he would have his piece of meat and then he would surreptitiously stick it under his cloak and off he'd go.

In late 1943 the Yanks arrived in preparation for the D-Day landings. As kids we would all stand on the side of the road watching them and shout out, 'Got any gum, chum?' We had never seen chewing gum in the village before. It was a rare thing to have and occasionally they would chuck a bit of gum to you and, sometimes, the very generous ones would throw you a bar of chocolate, or candy as they called it.

The hub of the village had always been Maggie's chip shop,

which was run by our neighbours, the three sisters. You would go in and wait your turn, sitting on wooden benches at the back end of the shop, and above your head would be a shelf of Tizer or Dandelion and Burdock bottles. There would be fresh sawdust on the floor every day. You would be waiting your turn and think, 'There's only a few people in front of me,' when suddenly the door would open and the RAF boys would come in with an order of fish and chips for 20. Maggie used to say, 'Sorry, priority for the RAF boys.' And there we would be waiting another half an hour and then, when your turn finally came, the trolleybus would stop outside and the conductor would run in, with his leather bag in front of him with all the coins shaking, and say, 'Priority, priority, we've got to have two fish and chips straightaway because we can't be late at the next stop!' And we'd have to wait again.

While I failed to make the most of my academic opportunities in Stradey school my rugby education flourished. I hadn't really played the game before, apart from the run-arounds on the village field, but we were fortunate to have a teacher by the name of Tolstoy Henton. Although a history teacher Toy, as he was known, also introduced us to rugby. He was a small man with a big voice; you dare not confront him about anything because he really ruled the roost in the school.

Believe it or not I started my first ever game in the front row, even though I was the smallest in the team. Alongside me was John Beili who was twice my size. It was my introduction to bruises and after being mauled senseless I realised that it wasn't the place I wanted to be so I moved to scrum-half. I was far better suited to the position and played there for a while until Mr Henton realised that, despite being the smallest player in the team, I had the biggest kick; so he moved me to outside-half.

Over the course of my rugby career you could say that I earned a reputation for being a tough tackler. Believe it or not, that was evident even as a scrap of a schoolboy, with one incident particularly etched in the memory. Although parents would be horrified by such practice today, on occasions Mr Henton liked to join in with us on the field. Being that he was a little taller and heavier than us kids, he would grab the ball and set off down the touchline, with his trousers flapping away, shouting, 'Come on! Come on! Tackle me!'

And I did. I hit him one day so hard that he fell over and he couldn't breathe. It took him about ten minutes to come round. He looked at me and I thought, 'I'm in trouble here.'

But he didn't say anything. I later heard that he'd gone back to the staffroom afterwards and told the other teachers, 'That boy is going to play for Wales one day.' I was only 12 years of age.

There was another teacher in our school at the time, Hywel Thomas, who had played a couple of games for Llanelli. At lunchtimes he would invite me to help him practice his kicking. However, it always turned into a kicking dual. No matter where he kicked the ball I caught it. It was a source of huge frustration to him because I then kicked it back, with either foot, to where he stood. He later became chairman of Llanelli and I used to take great pleasure in reminding him of how a schoolboy out kicked him!

Again I think I may have inherited my kicking from my father. I was once told that on one occasion he was playing for Llanelli when his shot at goal hit the crossbar breaking it in half causing it to fall on top of the goalkeeper. He must have had one hell of a kick.

It was also around this time that I suppose you could say I helped develop the spiral or torpedo kick which, sadly, seems to be disappearing from today's game, with modern players opting for the shorter but safer end-over-end style. The idea came to me out of the blue. In those days the ball had lacing around where the valve was. I thought if I chop it slightly, the weight will carry it around in a spiral. I couldn't get it first of all but then I twigged it – I used to roll it off my foot from the side, and it went a hell of a length. I found that at the end of the kick I could turn it inwards, so I would spiral it along the touchline and then it would turn in. I used to do it off either foot.

In my final year at school I was selected to play for Llanelli Schoolboys at outside-half. The most thrilling part of it all was that the game was due to take place on the hallowed turf of Stradey Park. It was a dream come true.

Up until then my parents couldn't afford to buy me proper rugby boots, so I had been playing in an old pair of shoes that my father had adapted by fixing strips of leather across to stop them falling apart. But because of my selection they decided to reward me with my first proper pair. I will never forget how proud and excited I was going with my mother to Llanelli market to buy them. I felt like royalty.

I had butterflies in my stomach for a week before the game. Come the day, I was sat in the famous Stradey dressing room, awash with nerves and expectations, when Ossie Williams, a Llanelli and Wales player, stuck his head around the door to wish us all the best for the game. We were all lost for words; the great Ossie Williams had wished us luck!

If you are not familiar with Ossie Williams there is one story that summed the man up perfectly. He was one of the greatest back-row players ever to play for Llanelli. He was a very strong man indeed and captained Llanelli against South Africa in 1952.

The night before the game he was working in the local steelworks and there was a blast. He turned his back on the fire. When he took his shirt off the molten metal had gone down behind his belt and, by the time he got that off, it had formed a band of sores around his waist. He was told to go to the first-aid room but refused as he knew they would stop him playing the next day.

When it came to changing for the game he took his jersey

into the toilets to change. After the game he couldn't get his jersey off, they had to cut it into strips and peel it off as it had stuck to his body through the sores. That's what it meant to him to play for Llanelli.

The South African captain later said that Ossie was one of the hardest players he had ever played against.

When my time came to run out of that tunnel down Stradey, the hair on the back of my neck stood up and the atmosphere crackled. I realised that half the town must have been there, including most of Bynea. In those days there was very little entertainment besides watching rugby. The feeling that day has stayed with me all my life; it was only bettered when I ran out for the first time in a Welsh jersey with the three feathers on my chest.

That first game was against Neath Schools and we emerged winners, by 12 points to 5, after a tough encounter. Our reward was a trip to the Talbot Athletic ground to play Aberavon who we beat by 6 points to 3, before we hammered Ystradgynlais to land a semi-final spot against Swansea at Stradey Park. We were on a roll and beat our traditional rivals, 6–0. Following the game a little report appeared in the local newspaper saying, 'Terry Davies, the home fly-half, was easily the best back on the field.'

The final was against Cardiff and took place in Aberavon as it was seen to be a neutral venue halfway between the two places. Two memories stand out for me from that day. First, the weather was atrocious and the game really should have been abandoned, and second, we lost the game by one try scored by a flying winger called Billy Boston, who went on to become one of the all-time greats of rugby league.

Towards the end of that season I was picked to play in a Welsh Schoolboys' trial in Gowerton but the selectors didn't give me a look-in because I was the smallest boy on the field!

The following year, at the age of 14, I left school and entered the world of work. My first job was in the Vitraflex enamel works in Dafen where they made rainwater goods, such as gutters and drainpipes. I was paired with a chap called Walter Rees and our task was to take these red-hot pipes and S-bends, after they had come out of a big furnace, and transfer them to the lower end of the works, lay them on the floor, singly and gently because once you chipped them they would be seconds, in order for them to cool. We wore large leather gloves and an apron to guard against being burnt to a crisp.

After a few weeks I had found my feet and I realised that Walter, being a lot older than me in his 50s, used to get tired at the end of the day. So, in an effort to make it easier for him, I said, 'Walter, why don't you throw them to me?'

He just looked at me and said, 'What do you mean?'

'You just throw them and I'll catch them,' I explained, 'It will save us walking.'

So that's what he did. He threw them, hesitantly at first, about ten yards, and I caught them and laid them down gently. Before long word got around and other people working there used to come to see the spectacle.

Walter got so blasé about it that he didn't really care where I was; he would just throw them over his shoulder. Of course if you didn't manage to catch a red-hot six-foot pipe correctly you would be in trouble; you couldn't bring them into your body. Sometimes they would come awkwardly and I would catch it on the side of my face and have a burn; that was a real lesson to catch properly. I later realised that having gone through this process helped my rugby skills considerably. I would handle that wet ball with no problem at all, thanks to my days in the Vitraflex works.

One day the manager, Mr Jones, walked in and just stood there in amazement. Now Walter hadn't seen him and proceeded to distribute everywhere in his usual carefree manner; they came like a shower but I managed to catch everything while the manager stood there transfixed. Once we had finished I thought he was going to say something but he just turned and walked away. He never mentioned our unique technique but we later heard that he had told people in the office that he had seen something incredible.

My brother Len, who was 18 months older than me, also worked in the Vitraflex works. His role was to dip the pipes in the enamel before hanging them on an overhead circular track which went through the furnace. He had to work nights, which was difficult because he couldn't sleep in the day and always started nodding off in the early hours of his shift.

I worked at Vitraflex for two years until I was 16. It was a happy works but I was made redundant when the place closed – aluminium and a little bit of plastic came into being and that was the end of enamel goods.

I then went to work in the washery at the Mountain colliery in Gorseinon. It was a very wet and difficult job. I had big Wellingtons on and we used to clean out the washery pits when they silted up; a bit of a nasty job really. We used to have a little cabin where every Friday our foreman would put a shovel over a little coal fire, which we had going in a large tin, and he would slap some fish on it; you knew that it was a Friday when you smelt the fish frying on the shovel. It was also handy for corned beef sandwiches which would be grilled until they became toast and the corned beef soft and runny; man, it was a treat!

My last job before joining the Marines was as a plasterer's mate. At the time they were building a large council house estate in Llwynhendy. My job was to mix the plaster in this big mixer and then wheelbarrow it across into the houses. I had to keep two plasterers going and because they were on piecework, and I wasn't, they earned more the faster we worked but I didn't. Now that needled me. They were Swansea boys and when I wasn't quick enough they used to curse me. I quietly put up with it but I would have my revenge one day in the not too distant future.

As for my rugby I started playing for Bynea youth when I

turned 16 but was quickly selected for the club's first team. One youth game does stand out though, against Penclawdd, which was always a fearsome place to play. As a 13 year old I went to watch Bynea play our deadly rivals. In a very tight game, with Penclawdd leading by a point, our wing was running unopposed for a try when some old lady stepped out from the touchline and hit him with an umbrella!

On this occasion our local doctor, Dr Hughes, approached us to ask if his son could have a game for us. Now Rowland Hughes was home from Harrow public school where he proudly boasted that he had been playing in the first XV.

Rowland ran out immaculately dressed, even his shorts were pressed with a pleat in them! I was playing outside-half with Rowland in the centre. After ten minutes we had good clean ball and I passed to Rowland who charged down the middle of the field. Now for some unknown reason, he cut back into the middle of the forwards. There was one hell of a scuffle before Rowland appeared from the mêlée running back towards me with his previously immaculately groomed hair sticking up and eyes open wide in panic. I asked, 'Are you alright, Rowland?' To which he replied, 'My God! They don't play like this in Harrow.'

Shortly after that game I was selected for the first team. It was quite a thing playing alongside and against grown men in their 30s at such a young age but you soon learned a bit about life. As a 16 year old I didn't drink and after the game I would sit and watch while they had a good sing-song and a good drink together; that kind of camaraderie made rugby so special back then, even at the highest level of the game. Sadly I think it has been lost today.

Just before Christmas I found myself selected to play for a west Wales XV in a game against Neath at the Gnoll. Although we were easily outplayed and lost the game 18–0, the newspapers were very kind to me the next day:

The most dangerous man on the field was undoubtedly wing-three-quarter John Huins. He crossed the line twice but would have done so on at least two other occasions had he not been magnificently tackled by the young Bynea fullback Terry Davies. This lad came out of a trying ordeal with flying colours, his sense of positioning being first-class.

Another newspaper picked up on my tackling of the Neath wing, John Huins:

Chief of these Huins stoppers was fullback Terry Davies (Bynea) whose slight build belied the power which he put into his crash tackles of Huins. Davies, a good all round fullback, certainly stopped several tries by getting Huins down.

Despite the accolades it was a case of back to Bynea where I finished off my first season in the first team with an end-of-season treat. The club arranged a trip to Lampeter as a kind of thank you to everybody for playing for the club. On our way home we had a chap sitting at the front of the bus because he wasn't feeling very well, having drunk too much. We had to stop for him to be sick just outside of the town. He eventually climbed back on board and we made our way home. Then, the next day, he realised that when he had been sick he had lost his false teeth. He jumped on his bike and cycled all the way back to Lampeter, only arriving home after dark, but with his teeth!

CHAPTER 4

Branded a traitor in
my own village

THE RIVALRY BETWEEN Swansea and Llanelli on the rugby
field is right up there with the most bitter grudge matches in
the world of sport; never mind Celtic and Rangers, the Jacks
and the Turks truly hate each other.

There are many versions of how Swansea came to be
labelled the Jacks and Llanelli became known as the Turks.
I like to believe that the true answer was related to me as a
boy by my grandfather. Some say the term Jacks derived from
the famous dog, Swansea Jack, who saved 20-odd people
from drowning in the docks in the 1920s, but my grandfather
disagreed.

'You know that the Jacks name didn't originally come from
the dog, it came from the fact that old Jack Crow would eat all
the bread but leave the crumbs!' he said. That's how the Port
Talbot and Llanelli dockers used to view the Swansea Jacks.

He told me a story of a time when two ships carrying pig
iron from Turkey arrived at Swansea Docks. Now Swansea
dockers were notorious for not wanting any heavy work, only
doing the light, easy tasks and getting well paid for it. The pig
iron would have to be manhandled several times, and it was
very heavy work indeed, so the dockers approached the ships'
captains and demanded more money before carrying out the
work. They were rebuffed and a stand-off occurred. The ships
sat in the docks with their cargo on board until somebody
from Llanelli heard of the problem and managed to convince

the Turkish captains that they would be better off coming to Llanelli, which they did. Now the Swansea dockers thought that they had been double-crossed and from that day on they called the Llanelli people Turks, out of a grudge.

My grandfather added, 'When the Jacks got rich from eating up all the best work, they got a bit toffee-nosed and wanted to change the name of the bird, so they decided to call themselves the Swans, or the lily-whites, because that made them feel better!'

I mention this rivalry because I found myself in the middle of it at the start of my second season of senior rugby when, at the age of 17, I was invited to play for Swansea. Apparently, with my name cropping up in the sports pages of the newspapers, and my performance in that game against Neath for the west Wales XV, I had come to the attention of the St Helen's side's selectors.

When I said yes, uproar ensued. For a Llanelli boy to go and play for Swansea in those days was virtually treason; you were branded a traitor. Very few players from this side of the Loughor Bridge ever went to play for the Jacks and I took some stick I must admit. However there was sound logic to my decision because Gerwyn Williams, the incumbent Welsh fullback at that time, was playing for Llanelli, so there was no opportunity for me at Stradey Park. Swansea were a very good side with some great internationals playing for them and, along with Cardiff and Newport, I suppose they were one of the top teams in Wales. I had to take the opportunity and I accepted it gratefully. Incidentally, I received an offer to play for Neath on the same day but, as history testifies, I turned them down.

My first game for the Whites was up in Ebbw Vale which is not an easy place to get to today let alone in the 1940s! Being so young my father came along with me. We set off early on the Saturday morning, caught the service bus from Bynea to Swansea and made our way to the old police station, on Orchard Street in the town centre, to board the team bus. When I arrived there was a gentleman who was in charge of getting everybody on to the bus.

I asked, 'Is this the Swansea bus?'

'It's the players' bus, the supporters' bus is the next one over there,' he replied pointing to another bus behind.

I said, 'I'm not a supporter, I'm playing for Swansea.' He looked at me and I could see in his eyes that he was thinking, 'What the hell have we got here?'

That bus journey was a little bit embarrassing because I was a bad traveller – I only had to look at a bus and I felt sick. I had to stop the bus twice before we had even reached the heads of the valley. I could see the apprehension of some of the Swansea selectors and could imagine them thinking, 'We've picked a schoolboy and now he's bloody sick again.' But I managed to survive until we finally arrived in Ebbw Vale. After sucking in a bit of fresh air I changed and went out onto the field.

Ebbw Vale had an impressive unbeaten home ground record stretching back for almost a year, and it was typical valley weather, quite misty with lots of rain, but, lo and behold, we won the game 6–0.

The selectors needn't have worried as the headlines in the newspaper the next day proclaimed:

Swansea has found the next international fullback.

Another read:

Davies even surprised veteran watchers by coolness under pressure, faultless fielding and lengthy touch-finding. He did not put a foot wrong throughout a fierce game.

I was very much in favour after that debut and shortly afterwards found myself playing against a Cardiff side packed full of internationals at the Arms Park. There was Haydn Morris on the wing, the centres were Bleddyn Williams and Jack Matthews, Gareth Griffiths on the other wing, with Frank

Trott at fullback, then you had Cliff Morgan at outside-half with Rex Willis at inside half; what a team. It was no surprise when we lost by around 28 points to 12, as we were slightly overwhelmed. Bleddyn Williams had a field day. I remember on one occasion Cliff Morgan had kicked a ball into no man's land just behind our defence, I attacked it, managed to gather and shot up the field. That was the last thing I remember because I was hit by the great Jack Matthews. It was a hell of a tackle and was like being hit by an Exocet missile. I was flattened and couldn't get my breath back. I was feeling sick and shaking all over. It took me several minutes to come round from it. It's funny because I referred to it years later and I said to Jack, 'Why didn't you show me mercy when I played in that game for Swansea? I was only 17 and you should have taken pity on me.'

He replied to me, 'My dear chap, I never recognise faces, only the colours of their jerseys.'

When you look at the money players are earning today, and how pampered they appear to be, I think back to a wing playing for us that season, a chap called Perris James from Caio near Lampeter. We used to train twice a week and he would get on his bike and ride from Caio to Lampeter, then come to Carmarthen by train and then from Carmarthen to Swansea. It used to take him around three hours. Then, after we'd finish training at about 8 o'clock, he would catch the 9 o'clock train back to Carmarthen and then back to Lampeter and cycle home. He wouldn't get back til about midnight. That was some journey and he used to do it twice a week and then again on the Saturday when we used to play. And that was all for 50p to buy drinks after the game. Now that's commitment for you.

Playing for the Whites was a real education in life. I was a naïve young lad coming from a small village, a closed village really, who knew nothing about life. I knew nothing about anything really. I came to Swansea and I really grew up because you had people who had fought in the war and had come back and started their careers again. Between their stories and their escapades, it was a pleasure to sit in a bus for about eight hours, going to Leicester or one of the other English teams, and you would sit there and listen. It was a huge thrill for me to just be there.

Now one of our players – who shall remain nameless – had the largest lunchbox you had ever seen in your life. It was so big his wife had knitted him this home-made jockstrap – she only had pink wool! – to accommodate him and even then he used to have to reel it up like a fireman's hose to get it inside.

We were playing against Cardiff, with 40,000 people packed into the St Helen's ground, when half-time arrived, in what was a very tough game. The trainer came on with a plate of sliced oranges, which was the norm in those days, and we gathered around in a circle. You had to be quick because if you didn't get to the oranges before the front five forwards there wouldn't be any left. As we were standing around in a circle discussing the game, I felt a nudge with an elbow to my side and this gentleman shook his leg and said to me, 'What do you think of this?' and his lunchbox was peeping out of his very long shorts down by his knees. He added, 'You know, I give it an airing in every game.' I think that must be some kind of record that is never going to be broken with all the television close-ups you see today!

Almost all the players liked to joke around and, still being a kid of 17, I was quite a menace myself. I would do silly things like putting Vaseline on doorknobs in the hotel so that when players went up to their rooms they couldn't get in and would have this wallop of Vaseline on their hands. However, my team-mates eventually became fed up with my games and decided to teach me a lesson. We were playing down in Plymouth on the end-of-season tour, and I must have done something really naughty because I felt hands grabbing me, taking every bit of clothing off me and seeing black boot polish and brushes.

I was black polished all over and, the worse thing of the lot, I was thrown into the restaurant of the hotel, which was full of people having their dinner at the time, and the door was shut tightly so that I couldn't get out. That caused quite a stir actually and it certainly stopped my messing about, well almost!

I was a bit of a joker with my friends from the village as well and one story, concerning a chap called Ken Lloyd, who was a great character and weighed around 17 stone, comes to mind. I was persuaded to join Ken and some other Bynea boys on a first proper holiday to Jersey. I remember sending a postcard home to my mother telling her that we were enjoying ourselves and Ken, who wasn't that good at writing, said. 'Can you send a postcard for me?'

It was one of those things that you become sorry for afterwards. I sent the postcard to Ken's mother and said that he'd met a lovely girl on holiday and would be bringing her home to meet them all. I just thought it was a bit funny. Of course, the day after we came back from our holidays, Ken came up to the house and said, 'What the hell did you do? My mother papered the whole bloody house thinking that I was bringing a girl home!'

My debut season in first-class rugby also saw me play against an international team for the first time, when the Springboks arrived in town in December 1951. As with all South African teams, they were really big and brutal. For a long period of time the 1951/52 Boks were rated one of the best touring teams ever to come to Great Britain. They only lost one match, out of 31, on the tour, with a weakened side against a London Counties team.

Basil Kenyon, their captain, had picked up an eye injury so the captaincy had been passed on to Hennie Muller, who was a big Number 8, much larger than any of our players, as was the whole team. Their front row was massive and one of them, Okey Geffin, who was about 18 stone, was their goal kicker. He had spent his time during the Second World War in a German prisoner of war camp. All he did during his internment was practice goal kicking for the whole period he was there; he could kick the ball from anywhere and was a top-class goal kicker.

Despite the disparity in size, and the fact we had three 18 year olds in our team, we gave them one hell of a game. We really took them to the wire and the scores were locked at 3–3 before it slipped away in the last eight minutes of the game. Their Number 8 Muller broke from behind the scrum and came down into our 25. As the last line of defence, I upended him but he managed to get the ball to their very good winger, a guy by the name of Chum Ochse who, despite his name, was no friend to us as he shot over in the corner. Geffin promptly put the conversion over. We eventually lost by 11 points to 3 but it had certainly been one of the hardest games they had had on tour.

The game is also memorable on a personal level because I learnt a very important lesson. Just before half-time they were attacking into our 25 (it was all yards in my day but is the 22-metre line now) when the ball was kicked ahead. I easily marked the ball and, in my naivety, I stood there and looked at an approaching forward, who was their hooker. I looked at him and thought, 'Oh well, the referee has blown his whistle so he's going to stop.' Well he didn't! I ended up about five yards away flat on my back. We had a penalty but it certainly knocked the stuffing out of me. After that I always remembered never to leave myself open after marking the ball; put your elbows up, put your foot up, put your studs in his face, it doesn't matter, just keep yourself well protected. That was a major lesson.

Around this time my brother Len was coming to the end of his National Service – he was with the Sappers in Chatham – and being an excellent rugby player himself he had been playing for various teams in the army. It so happened that he was back in south Wales on tour with his regimental side and, having picked up a few injuries, they were short of players, so my brother asked me if I would help out. I loved my brother, so there was no way that I would have said no. They were playing against Glamorgan Wanderers and had lost every game until then but, of course, we managed to beat them by 3 points to nil; I dropped a goal. After the game everybody wondered who this small Welsh player starring for the Engineers was; nobody had heard of him! Glamorgan Wanderers approached me and asked if I would join them when I left the army. Of course, I didn't tell them that I was already a Swansea player.

That was my first experience of playing for a military team but it wouldn't be my last. In fact, it was soon to become a regular occurrence.

CHAPTER 5

Life in the Royal Marines

I GREW UP at a time when men between the ages of 17 and 21 had to undertake their National Service. You were compelled to serve in a branch of the armed forces for two years and then remain on the reserve list for something like four years. There were exceptions, such as working underground or in agriculture, but being a rugby player wasn't one of them, so there was no getting around it.

I had given it a great deal of thought and decided to use it to my advantage and joined the Royal Marines. One of the reasons I stood out on the rugby field was my lack of size; at 5 feet 8 inches I was still quite slim, only weighing in at around 11 stone 10 pounds. I thought that the Marines, with their reputation for being quite a tough unit, would probably do me the world of good to help build my strength up and increase my size. It proved the right decision because I really enjoyed my time there and when I left I was 5 feet 11 inches and I had put on a stone and a half.

Before joining up I was still labouring for those two Swansea plasterers who had enjoyed exploiting me and making my life hell. However, I was to have my revenge on my last day. As the shift drew to an end I had a little slow period, I knew they would chastise me and, when I arrived with the last barrow, full to the brim, those Swansea boys were standing there telling me that I had lost them their bonus for the day.

I said, 'I don't care!' And I tipped the whole barrowful over them. I can still see them standing there speechless!

The Marines knew all about my rugby and just a week or so after making my way down to Lympstone near Exeter, to enrol, I was selected to play for the Royal Navy on their trip to Paris. There I was, in my uniform, taking in the sights and enjoying myself playing rugby; it was quite a start to life in the armed forces!

I remember I was very well treated but, at a time when the class system was still rife, I found it slightly unusual and off-putting being the only private in the team. They were a different group to me and I didn't know how to handle them. On the field some of them were very good players, especially a second row called Wilkinson who I think captained England later on in his career, but they came from a privileged background I knew nothing about.

It was something that I was to go on and notice when I played international rugby, a kind of inferiority complex inherent in us Welsh. When I played, the vast majority of the English, Scottish and Irish teams were made up of university types – no wonder they used to accuse the Welsh of sticking together on Lions tours.

When I returned from Paris ten days later I discovered, to my cost, that the camp hadn't been informed that I was playing for the Navy and I was listed down as being absent without leave! When I strolled through the gates at Lympstone, the sentry called the sergeant who said to me, 'You're missing. Where have you been?'

I replied, 'I've been to Paris with the Royal Navy rugby team.'

He looked me up and down and said, 'I've heard some stories in my time but that's the best one yet!'

I ended up sitting in a cell in the guard room, with the doors open and drinking cups of tea, while waiting to be released. After an hour or so the call came from the CO to get me out of the cells double-quick and back into training.

I really enjoyed my training in the Marines because it pushed you to the limits. I was already fit going in there, which was a huge bonus, but they took me to a whole new level. I found it pretty easy-going to be honest, much to the annoyance of our English sergeants who were training us. They liked to be the first at everything and I thoroughly enjoyed showing them up. I used to play on Saturdays for Devonport Services, and I was having a good life really, so there was a great deal of envy about it. As a result I found myself being tested rather harder at times than some of the other Marines, but I just sucked it up, as they say, and came out stronger.

One of the more brutal training exercises that we did were the speed marches. You would always start early in the morning before dawn and set off romping along in full kit. We started off doing three miles in 30 minutes but soon had to build up to six miles and then it increased to ten. You would run in formation and, unfortunately, being the fittest, I was always selected to be in the last four of the ten charging along, which meant after about six or seven miles, when some of the front runners would be tiring and failing, their kit would be passed back to lighten their load and I'd always end up with two rifles around my neck and somebody else's rucksack on my back.

I eventually became a pacemaker for officers coming back from abroad to retrain. You would always get the gung-ho ones who thought they were super fit, who would shout, 'Come on pacemaker; can't you go any quicker?!'

I would reply courteously, 'I can go as quick as you like, Sir.'

By the time we were coming to the end, they would be staggering around and there wasn't a peep from any of them.

Another testing training exercise was the night match where you had to traverse along a barren piece of Dartmoor, without a road in sight, and arrive at a set destination using your compass. It was carried out by ten of you, all starting off at different points. You set your compass, set off and you couldn't see a thing. Now to me, a country boy from a small village, I was more than at home in the dark but the same couldn't be said for most of the cocky city slickers amongst us. On one such exercise I was halfway along my track and about to come up to the brow of a long hill, when I heard a voice in the distance singing. I thought, 'It must be one of the boys.' I decided to have a bit of fun and so I lay down.

I could hear him walking towards me and, as he passed I suddenly jumped up. Well, I had never heard anyone shout and scream so much in my life. He was shouting and screaming all the way over the next hill and on out of sight and sound.

Still smiling to myself, I made my way to the collection point and climbed in the back of the lorry waiting to collect us. The conversation all the way back to the camp was of this chap having seen a ghost. I thought I had better not say anything as I would be in trouble. From that night on those city slickers wouldn't cross the moor at night without fixing bayonets first!

Now anyone who has trained seriously will know that it takes more than lots of exercise to build yourself up and that diet plays an equally important role. I was lucky in that I found a friend and ally in the form of fellow Welshman John Collins, who happened to be strategically placed in the kitchens.

Now John could shift; he played on the wing for Aberavon and would go on to represent Wales on the track, but how the hell he managed to get into the Marines I could never work out because he couldn't see a thing without his thick pebble glasses. On the rugby field, when he didn't wear his glasses, he didn't know which side the try line was and you would occasionally have to point him in the right direction.

Thankfully, they soon realised that they couldn't trust John with guns so they gave him a job in the cookhouse. That suited me perfectly because he was able to subsidise my diet. Before making our training runs you would have to go down to the mess to pick up a packed lunch. Now this was usually two pieces of bread with an inch-thick layer of marmalade in the middle and one boiled egg, which, when peeled, was black. I didn't fancy these so I used to go without and come back into camp about 4 o'clock starving because I hadn't eaten anything. John was really in the right place because I used to nip around to the back of the cookhouse and ask, 'John, have you got anything to eat?' Invariably he would keep me a slice of pie or something that helped me along greatly.

One day, however, I went around the back to find John sitting on this milking stool in front of a huge galvanised bowl with around a ton of potatoes in it. He was tasked with peeling and taking the eyes out of every one of those potatoes.

I said, 'How are you today?' Well, the language was dreadful. He didn't want that job, he'd been there all day, he was going to desert the Marines, and he was going to bugger off home and to hell with everybody!

I said, 'Cool down John, you don't want to be doing a silly thing like that.'

He replied, 'I've had it with them. Look at all those that I've got to do again!' There was another pile next to the first.

Trying to change the subject, and without much expectancy, I said, 'Well, is there anything for me today?'

'Bugger all!' he replied.

I could see that he was in a stroppy mood and there would be no getting around him so I started walking away trying to console myself with the fact tea would be served in around three hours and that it would be egg and chips, with the prospect of a second helping of chips.

However, I had only gone a few steps when John called after me, 'By the way Terry, I wouldn't be having the chips tonight.'

I turned back and asked, 'Why not?'

'Because I've bloody well pissed all over them!'

To be honest with you I was so hungry I did have chips that night and I did have second helpings. When needs must, and you're starving, you'll do anything.

CHAPTER 6

First Cap

SATURDAY, 17 JANUARY 1953, is a day I will never forget as it saw me achieve the dream of almost every schoolboy in Wales – playing for your country.

It was unexpected as I was so young, just 19, but despite being picked in the Possibles – as opposed to the Probables – in the final Welsh trial in Cardiff, I helped the white jerseys beat the reds comprehensively by 27 points to 9.

The newspaper said the next day:

> The star performer of the match was undoubtedly Terry Davies whose tackling, kicking and general play was really great.

Another newspaper called it 'a flawless performance', so I must have deserved my call-up.

It was the first Five Nations international of the season and being against England in Cardiff made it even more special. I had made the long journey home from Plymouth on the Thursday, arriving quietly in Bynea late in the evening, where I enjoyed a little celebration with my family. It was a bit surreal trying to comprehend my call-up while on the base; coming home made it more real. And then there were all the well wishes from close friends and neighbours, along with the telegrams including the very first one I received from Dr Hughes the village doctor, whose son had played alongside me against Penclawdd. I've still got that tucked away in one of my cuttings books.

On the Friday I caught the train to Cardiff to meet up with the team. We had lunch in the Angel Hotel followed by a team run at one of the university grounds in the capital for an hour or so before heading back home in time for tea – a world away from the intense training camps of today but exciting nonetheless.

We didn't have a coach back then and the Big Five and WRU (Welsh Rugby Union) committee rarely left the bar, so it was left up to us to organise ourselves. The captain usually played the lead and, if he was a forward, us backs were left to do our own thing.

Of course the game was far less structured than you see today, with far more room to express yourself, and we generally relied upon individual flair to win through. That night, despite being back in my old bedroom, I didn't get a wink of sleep; it's an unavoidable fact that you are not able to sleep the night before your first international.

I got up early the next morning and my mother had been to the market to get me some cockles and laverbread to go with my bacon and egg. Then it was off to the bus stop to catch the bus into Swansea where I was to board the 9.30am train to Cardiff. Tickets really were like gold dust in those days, and the WRU only gave you two, so they were given to my proud parents. Sadly, my brothers and sisters had to miss out.

When I got off the bus at Swansea's High Street station I was greeted with the astonishing sight of around 2,000 people milling about. It was just a sea of flat caps moving around in waves, so tightly packed, you couldn't put your nose in there.

Fortunately, there was a compartment on the train reserved for the players making their way from Swansea but we were ogled all the way to Cardiff. Everybody would come up and try and get in to talk to you. It was simply a mad train journey.

Once we arrived in Cardiff we struggled to make our way back to the Angel Hotel through an even bigger mass of flat caps; I had never seen anything like it. After a light lunch we made our way across Westgate Street to the ground, the Arms Park, and as we reached the players' entrance the crowd parted like the Red Sea to allow us inside.

The East Stand dressing room was quiet, nobody had much to say, all were preoccupied with their own thoughts and rituals. Then came a magic moment when the jersey was handed to me by the trainer. What a thrill, I couldn't take my eyes off it. I remember the great Newport wing Ken Jones, who was a real teaser, coming over to me and saying, 'That's your first jersey, good boy.'

'Yes,' I said proudly staring at it in my hands.

'Now listen to me,' Ken continued, 'If Dai Jones the selector offers you a boiled sweet after the game, don't take it because it means you're dropped.' Now I believed every word and I avoided Dai Jones and his boiled sweets after each game that season like the plague until the penny finally dropped – he was just having a laugh.

As quiet as the players were, there was a terrific noise coming from the stands above. You could hear the singing, you could hear the feet stomping on the wooden boards; it was one huge wall of noise washing down to the dressing room.

Once the referee gave the signal we had to run out through the back entrance and along the walkway right around the Arms Park until we got to the other side. We clip-clopped and waited underneath the West Stand before running out. The noise was indescribable, it shook the whole stand, and then it was time to go. When you ran onto the field, in front of that immense crowd, with everybody roaring, shouting and screaming, your head was buzzing and the hairs on the back of your neck were standing on end, your chest puffed out – what a feeling, what a great, great feeling that was! It wasn't a once-in-a-lifetime experience; every time I put the jersey on the same priceless feeling of pride in playing for my country came back.

As I ran out, there was a youngster on the halfway line who was to become a good friend of mine, Denzil Griffiths, and he was holding two giant leeks. They were six feet high and I'm quite sure that Max Boyce must have remembered this because he took it up afterwards. Denzil, who eventually became the mayor of Tenby, was at every game with his giant leeks.

I don't remember much about the game itself because, even though it sounds like a cliché, it really did fly by so quickly; you couldn't catch up with it at times. I know I kicked a penalty in the first half and it soared through the posts but we never got near the English try line and they ran out winners by 8 points to 3. In our defence, all the papers had described the England team as the best since the war, which sounds impressive today, but back then it was only eight years! When the final whistle went it was a huge disappointment to me because I thought I hadn't done anything in the game and I was very frustrated. Quite early on in the first half I fell on a loose ball and the giant English wing, Woodward, put his boot into my side and cracked a rib for me. It was strapped up but it was difficult to get my breath and I ended the game a bit on the breathless side. Some of the papers described me as heroic for playing on through the pain but I didn't feel that way; there were no substitutes allowed in those days and I didn't want to let anybody down.

One newspaper wrote:

> Hero of the rugby international at Cardiff was young fullback Terry Davies. Hurtling himself at the feet of the hefty Woodward he damaged himself after quarter of an hour. From then on he was in agony, yet not once did he let his country down. Yesterday he could hardly walk.

The repercussions and inquests began in earnest but I was lucky in a way because I had to go back to the Marines on the Sunday and avoided the recriminations of all your friends and members of the public. 'Why did you lose? What went wrong? What happened?'

To be honest with you, I felt as though I should look for Dai Jones and ask for a boiled sweet because I thought I would be dropped for the next game. Thankfully, when the team was announced for the trip to Edinburgh to face Scotland, my name came out first again, although I had to pass a fitness test on my injured rib 24 hours before the game.

We travelled up by train in those days which meant a ten- or 11-hour trip. I came home on the Wednesday evening and caught the train at Swansea on the Thursday. Talk about a gravy train. Besides the players, there were around a hundred Welsh committee members and their wives on board. They sat in the front of the train while us players had the cheap seats in the back. The buffet car was in the middle and, of course, they would eat first and when it came to our turn there was hardly anything left. They'd scoffed the lot really, that's just the way it was. I remember a gentleman by the name of Tommy Vile, who, despite his name, was about the only one who used to talk to the players. He took a shine to me and we used to have good conversations. I was complaining to him that most of the food had been eaten and he looked at me and said, 'It's all down to importance. We are the important ones, the administrators, because we'll be here long after you've gone.' So what's really changed in the WRU?!

Vile, who was in his 70s, was a very interesting man as he'd been on the British Lions tour to New Zealand in the very early 1900s. He told me that they'd travel by boat, then by a wagon train of stagecoaches. When it was raining and the road became muddy, they'd all have to get out and help push the stagecoaches up the hills. At certain times, when the Maoris were restless, they would have a compliment of Red Coats to keep them safe.

The WRU was famously tightfisted in my day, we even had to buy our own programmes. They were a shilling each, so I haven't got a great collection at home.

Later in my career I would be asked to do some radio work for BBC Radio Wales on occasions. I would go down to the studio in Swansea, on Alexandra Road, and work with the broadcaster Eic Davies, who, incidentally was the father of Huw Llywelyn Davies who has followed in his father's footsteps. I remember little Huw, who was only around seven, sitting quietly in the corner taking it all in.

I would be paid £3 for my efforts but then I had to hand it over to the WRU who, in turn, would give me one and sixpence for my bus fare! There was no way you could get out of it. It was just a sign of the times. If you went to rugby league for example, you would be ostracised. You would be a pariah. I would often be enjoying a drink after the game in a packed clubhouse only to go home and find a little note pushed into my pocket saying, 'If you want to go North, call me.' Even the scouts were wary and wouldn't approach you in public.

The Big Five made eight changes to the side for the Scottish game, bringing a lot of experience back in with players like John Gwilliam and Rhys Stevens. Bleddyn Williams was the captain. He was one brilliant centre, one of the best jinkers off either foot I have ever seen. He would be three feet away, jink, and leave you stranded. He was also a good captain having been a glider pilot during the war. He had some very interesting stories of crossing over the English Channel on D-Day with 40 or so soldiers in the back, their weight making the glider almost uncontrollable. Talk about leading your troops into battle!

The Scottish game was a torrid affair. When we ran onto the field there was a huge open terrace, which held around 20,000 people. The noise coming off this was tremendous and your ears were blasted by it; it felt like you would be sucked into the crowd. Scotland were a kicking team and employed countless high up-and-unders, which their rampaging pack used to chase down. You couldn't hear yourself think, let alone play. Their outside-half would kick it up into the sky and I would be waiting for it to come down, with that roar and the sound of stampeding Scottish forwards coming closer. I had to shut the place off completely and just concentrate on catching the ball. I must have had a reasonable game that day because I was carried off the field shoulder high and there was a great photograph of somebody plonking a Welsh hat on my head in the newspaper the following day.

We had avenged a heavy defeat from the previous visit to Murrayfield two years earlier by winning 12–0 through three tries and a penalty, which I put over.

Again the press were kind to me:

> Another player deserving mention is the young fullback Terry Davies. Against the quick Scottish forwards he often came under heavy pressure but he remained cool and steady and showed that he can kick equally well with either foot.

Unlike a fortnight earlier it was a pleasure to get to the railway station on the Sunday with the cheering Welsh crowds. I could only imagine what the boys felt like two years previously when they'd been hammered by the Scots.

Another thing that sticks out from that trip is the renaming of one of our players, who shall remain nameless here. It's funny how people get nicknames. One of our front row forwards had negotiated with one of the chambermaids to meet him at 10 o'clock in his room. Of course the drinks were free after the game and he got so inebriated that he couldn't really do anything and the maid was heard saying 'Do you want me to give you a few wee jerks to help you along?' Of course, he became known as 'wee jerks' after that!

Ireland were up next and were in confident mood having drawn with England in their previous game. It was a memorable game for a number of reasons, not least because it was played in Swansea, on my home ground. St Helen's was regularly used for home internationals up until 1954, with games being shared with the Arms Park in Cardiff.

The game is also to be remembered for being the last time the great Jack Kyle pulled on the green jersey against Wales, as he was playing in his farewell season for Ireland. I remember him being a short, thick-set player with fair hair, who was one of the all-time greats of Irish rugby. As outside-half I must admit that on the day he had me running around in circles for about 20 minutes but then I twigged the way he was playing and I pre-empted and, from then on, nullified all his kicks.

St Helen's was a difficult field to play on because the pitch wasn't quite square to the far terrace. It ran at an angle towards the big bank opposite the grand wooden stand on the Oystermouth Road side, which was full to capacity, and when you were kicking towards touch you could never spot the touchline. But I'd played two seasons for Swansea, so I knew the ground and I think that helped greatly.

We came out winners by five points to three in quite a tight game. It's a terrific feeling being on the winning side because there is no inquest and everyone is pleasant to you.

Now something unusual happened on the Sunday morning after the Irish game. I was back in Bynea in my bed having a lie-in – I was due to catch the 9pm train from Llanelli to travel through the night back to Plymouth – when there was a knock on the front door. Then I heard my mother rushing up the stairs to my bedroom. She said, 'Quick, you've got to come down, there's three people asking for you and they've got very funny accents.'

I dressed quickly and went downstairs to the front door to discover the three gentlemen were rugby league scouts from Wigan. They had come down especially to see the Irish game as, apparently, the great Jim Sullivan had retired and they were looking for a replacement, and they thought that I was that replacement.

I asked them in quickly before anyone saw them because if the WRU got wind that I had been speaking to rugby league scouts they would have banned me from playing for life. I was pleasant enough and offered them a cup of tea, which my mother prepared in the best china, and we sat around the table in the parlour. My mother and father went out to the kitchen, the door slightly ajar because you know what parents are like, they want to know what was going on.

To be honest I was very curious because, with players, there is always this thing that you wanted to know how much they were prepared to pay for you; you wanted to know your value to them. I didn't have to wait very long. Suddenly this chap said to me. 'We would like to sign you for Wigan. We'll give you very good terms.'

I said, 'I'm sorry, I'm not interested. I'm in the forces now and might think about it in the future but certainly not now at the beginning of my career.'

Then he nodded to the second chap who had an attaché case, which he opened and tipped £5,000 in notes onto the table. Now I'd never seen more than a £5 note in my life. If I had a fiver I was quite rich. The Marines' pay was 17/6 a week and I used to send ten shillings home to my mother so, in reality, my weekly pay was £1.25, yet right then I was staring at £5,000 in very large notes. I looked at them and I thought, 'No, I'm not ready to go yet.'

My mother and father were looking through the half closed door and their mouths were down to the floor. They'd never seen that amount of money in their lives, either. My father's pay would have been about £3.50 to £4 a week. My mother said, 'Arglwydd Mawr,' and promptly fainted. Fortunately, my father managed to catch her just before she hit the floor.

Finally, I found my voice and said, 'The answer is still no.'

There was another nod and they went up to £9,000, which is close to £250,000 in today's money. It was lucky that my mother was too dazed to realise how much was now on the table!

I stuck to my guns and they saw that they were wasting their time and left.

I later learned that they went straight to Cardiff and signed a certain lad called Billy Boston who had scored the winning try in the Dewar Shield final when I was playing for Llanelli Schoolboys. Of course, Billy went on to enjoy great success up North, becoming one of the biggest legends of the game.

It doesn't end there, however, as many years later I was at a dinner in Swansea where he was the guest speaker. Afterwards I related the story. He remembered the three gentlemen vividly, and when I had finished he said, 'The bastards got me for £3,000. What a bargain!'

I have often thought about my decision that day because with £9,000 in 1953 I could have bought several small farms or about fifteen houses in Llanelli. Fortunately, when I reflect on that, I must admit that I am pleased that I turned it down because I thoroughly enjoyed my life in rugby. It would have been a shame had I gone North. I would have squandered the money. It would have been spent on cars and wild women as I suppose that was my nature in those days. I must admit that I wouldn't have met my wife and wouldn't have had the family I have now, so I'm very happy I didn't take the money.

The final game of the championship was away to France. We took the train down to Dover and then a boat across the Channel and then on to Paris. Unfortunately, it was a wild day and everybody was seasick but none more so than Clem Thomas, who would be seasick on a pedalo. As soon as we left the shelter of the harbour, he turned as green as a leprechaun and I'd never seen anybody be so sick in all my life, but at least it stopped him talking for a while! He was a tremendous orator and had such a way with words but, mind you, he was the only gentleman I knew who could speak Welsh with a Cambridge accent.

We got to Paris late on Thursday night and did a bit of training on the Friday and then it was a trip to the Folies Bergère. It was really pushing it, before an international, to go and look at the exotic follies, but that's what we did.

We played in the Stade Colombes on a bright spring day. The crowd, with its usual manic noises coming from all over the ground, was caged in by an eight-foot-high wire fence that ran around the pitch – no doubt to prevent wild Frenchmen running on to attack you! It was quite an experience.

One of the biggest characters in our team was a policeman from somewhere in the valleys called D M Davies. He was the roughest character I had ever seen. He had had lumps kicked out of him and was the closest thing I have seen to a real life Grogg. D M and I changed next to each other. I was ready within a few minutes but D M had to go through his pre-match ritual; first he put a bandanna on, and then he scooped up a big handful of Vaseline, which he smeared all over his forehead and cheeks, then he began putting it on his knees. As he was doing this I said, 'There's no need to put it on your knees, the pitch is soft.'

He looked at me and replied, 'Listen now good boy, when I'm knocking those Frogs' heads I don't want to skin my knees.'

Then it was the horse liniment, which was handy in winter to keep you warm but the smell was horrific. It used to permeate through your clothes and, of course, if you went to a dance afterwards you wondered why you were standing alone. And if you got any of it onto your privates you would have given Linford Christie a run for his money towards the toilet to dangle everything in. Now D M was stuffing it everywhere; he didn't blink an eyelid, he just splashed it on. It was amazing sight altogether.

It was quite a fast and open game and, with the sun on our backs, both our forwards and backs played well enabling us to run out winners by six points to three, thanks to two tries either side of half-time by the Cardiff wing, Gareth Griffiths.

After the match the French played hosts as only they can and we went to dinner at a top-class hotel called Hôtel Lutetia where the Queen stayed when she came over to Paris. It had a magnificent banqueting hall where we were served an elaborate five-course meal prepared by some of the finest chefs in France. I've never seen anything as good since and, at the end of the banquet, the lights were dimmed and a succession of waiters came in with the sweet, which was a kind of a see-through ice cream made into elephant and giraffe shapes all lit up with sparklers; it was a spectacular sight to see. Unfortunately, as one of the waiters came down the aisle he tripped and this elephant flew over the table and there was a scattering of ice cream everywhere.

It was not normal for me to drink so much but I had had quite a few celebratory drinks when Clem Thomas had an idea. We had an old sing-song routine in our Swansea days together, which was called 'This Old Coat of Mine'. You would be in the middle of the dance floor and someone would sing 'This Old Coat of Mine', then suddenly your coat would come off and your shirt would come off too. You would peel yourself down to your underwear. Clem said to me, 'Come on. We'll do the old song.' Off we went, the two of us, and grabbed the microphone on the stage. Clem took his coat off and I took my coat off. Then Clem took his shirt off and mine came off. Then came the trousers and shoes and, before we knew it, we were standing in our birthday suits on stage. We had a good laugh and didn't think anything more about it.

However, around three days after arriving home a brown envelope arrived for me from my old pal Vivian Jenkins, who was living out in Paris. When I opened it there were some clippings of Clem and I stark naked on the front of the French papers. He said we had been in the French papers the whole week!

And, of course, there was also an article referring to it in the *Western Mail*, by the renowned rugby writer J G B Thomas. My mother was furious and she said, 'You've let yourself down!' I received a real rocketing from my parents but Vivian Jenkins said in his letter, 'They've had record sales of the paper all week!'

I thoroughly enjoyed my first season of international rugby and it was exhilarating having played alongside my heroes; people like the Number 8 John Gwilliam, Bleddyn Williams, Ken Jones and Billy Williams. We had a good crowd of boys.

It was disappointing to have lost to England but three victories from four saw us finish runners-up to England by a point. It was not a bad return, especially when you consider that despite Wales having enjoyed massive success with two Grand Slams, in 1950 and 1952, to use a phrase common today, a rebuilding process was taking place. It would be a couple of decades, and the emergence of the likes of Gareth Edwards and Barry John, before we hit those kind of heights again.

CHAPTER 7

Going out
with a Bump!

ALTHOUGH THE FIVE Nations was over I was to play in another high profile tournament of sorts that season where the bragging rights were contested just as fiercely – if you were in the Armed Forces, that is.

The British Army has been playing rugby against the Royal Navy annually since 1907 and following the formation of the Royal Air Force, during the First World War, the RAF entered the equation in 1920 to form what is known today as the Inter-Services Championship. It takes place at the end of the season in Twickenham and, as you can imagine, there is always an awful lot of pride at stake, and the place was full to the brim when we played there in 1953.

First up was the RAF and this game, which we drew 3–3, stands out for me because, believe it or not, it was the first time I actually met Carwyn James. Not only was he a team-mate that day, but we took each other's positions. I was selected to play outside-half and there was Carwyn playing fullback. It was a funny situation because I hadn't met Carwyn before but I'd heard of him and knew that his natural position was at outside-half. I tried to explain this to the selector, who was a commander of some sort with the most braiding I'd ever seen on someone's shoulders. I said, 'I think you've got it wrong, Sir.'

He just looked down his nose at me and said, 'Are your querying my decision Davies?' Once again, as the only non-commissioned officer in sight, I thought I had better shut up and let him get on with it.

On the RAF side that day, playing in the second row, was a certain Rhys Williams, known as R H, another player who I didn't know at that time but he would become one of my best friends in rugby, playing alongside me for club, country and the Lions.

Prior to the series I had played in a warm-up game for the Navy in Portsmouth and had run into a friend of mine from Bynea called Des Bowen who was also doing his National Service at the time. I had managed to get a spare ticket for the game and decided to see if I could get Des to come along for a good day out. I went to his camp and the sentry at the gate directed me to a row of wooden huts. I knew I needed to come up with a good excuse in order for the plan to work and decided to tell them that Des was my brother, who I hadn't seen in months, and I had called on the off chance we may be allowed to spend the day together. With both of us being Welsh I thought it just might work.

I arrived at the correct hut to find a sergeant and around 20 soldiers writing away merrily at desks. Des was not a fighter, and proof that the pen is mightier than the sword.

The sergeant looked me up and down in my 42 Commando uniform and said, 'Can I help you?'

I said, 'Would you let my brother out for the day? I'm playing for the Royal Navy at Portsmouth and I took the opportunity to come here to see if you could let him come along?'

Now Des was only about 5 feet 4 inches and lucky to be 8 stone soaking wet so when the sergeant shouted, 'Bowen, come here!' we looked like Little and Large.

However, the sergeant allowed Des to go and we had a good time together; two Bynea boys hundreds of miles from home.

The next game in the Inter-Services Championship, against the Army, was the biggest of the lot. Being at Twickenham, a royal party was in attendance in the form of Princess Elizabeth – she had not yet been crowned – and her new husband Prince Philip. We lined up to greet them and I was passed by very quickly by the future queen but Prince Philip stopped and looked me up and down before asking, 'How old are you?'

I said, '18, Sir.'

He replied, 'You look bloody 15. But there we are, you've got the legs of an 18 year old.' And off he went.

On the other side that day, playing fullback for the Army, was Arthur Edwards who would go on to win a couple of caps for Wales. He was also a Bynea boy and it was nice to have a few words after the game, which was very tough indeed.

Sadly, we lost 3–0 but what stands out most of all is how obeying orders got me into a spot of bother. There was a huge up-and-under and, as the ball was coming down, there were quite a few players better positioned than myself but the voice of one of the officers in the side boomed out, 'Your ball, Davies!'

I thought, 'That's a command, I've got to take.' And I did and I took all the Army pack as well! I really was shunted about, you know.

Another example of the snobbery that existed in the services at that time was when Devonport Services, which was my regular side, were due to play against Cheltenham. We had a good few injuries, so the lieutenant commander, who was in charge of the team, said to me, 'Davies, there are quite a few out injured, so will you be captain for the day?'

I said, 'Yes, no problem.'

However, as we were changing in the dressing room he came back and said, 'I'm awfully sorry old chap but would you mind terribly standing down as captain because we've got seven officers on the team and they're quite opposed to you being captain as a private.'

As I have said, I was learning a lot about the wider world and people in general.

I got my own back, however, in a manner that would help my village club out tremendously. I had been back home for a rare bit of leave and Dai Nicholas, then the Secretary of Bynea, said that the club was thinking about starting a second XV but they couldn't do it because they couldn't afford a new set of jerseys. Now I thought about this after the Cheltenham game and a plan started to form in my mind. After games we used to gather all the jerseys and shorts and socks and put them in this old kit bag which, on away trips, would be taken off the bus near our home ground and thrown over a wall, and be picked up the next day to be taken to the laundry. On this particular occasion, however, I went over the wall myself the next day, retrieved the kit bag, got a bus down to the railway station, put a big label on it with string and stamps that cost nine shillings ten pence, and posted it by train to David Nicholas, care of Bynea RFC.

There was a bit of a fuss when they found out that our kit had gone missing but there was always plenty of money in the services for sports facilities, so they didn't really miss it. I just wished that I had been there to see Bynea Seconds running out for their first ever game dressed in smart blue jerseys, white shorts and blue socks.

After the season ended I underwent a selection of another kind, to do with the Coronation of Queen Elizabeth. They wanted fifty elite Marine Commandos to line the area around the Cenotaph in Whitehall on the big day and I was roped in. We practised standing to attention for six weeks and it was one of the most laborious times of my life. We just stood there for an hour the first day but, by the end of the week, we were standing for up to three hours, doing the 'Present arms' and all the drills. It was very tiring but we were building up to standing for ten hours.

When you stand there with nothing else to do for that length of time your mind wanders and if you don't 'Present arms' at the right time you find yourself having to run around this huge field, which was next to the parade square, holding the rifle above your head. I thought that this was great and every day I deliberately missed the 'Present arms' so I was sent around the field. Not only did I enjoy it more than standing still, it also kept me fit!

Unfortunately, the sergeant soon twiggcd what I was up to and said, 'I know what you're doing Davies; the next time you do it it's the cookhouse for an hour in the evening cleaning the utensils!' So that put paid to that.

The training over, we travelled up to London on 2 June 1953, the day of the Coronation. We were out there at 7.30am and lined up by the Cenotaph, opposite the Parliament buildings. It was an immense day altogether and when all those carriages, carrying royalty and heads of state from around the Commonwealth, passed, we were just yards away. We saw Princess Elizabeth pass us twice; the second time she had become our Queen and was on her way home. It was a marvellous day; the place was full, with crowds and crowds everywhere. The kids were allowed to come right up to your feet to have a look at the carriages passing by. I must admit that whatever else this country is, it can certainly put on the pomp and ceremony when it's needed; we must be the envy of the world.

The downside, as far as we were concerned, was that it went on and on! We had to stand to attention for the whole day; even when they were in Westminster Abbey we had to stand there rigidly. It got a bit boring as nothing was passing and I remember counting all the tiles on the Parliament housing on the other side of the street. I counted up to 3,451 tiles, which I remember to this day.

Following so many highs, winning my first cap, representing the Navy at Twickenham and being part of the Guard of Honour at the Queen's coronation, I was literally brought back down to earth with a bump when I fell into a trench in the dark, while on a Commando exercise, and dislocated my shoulder. I set off for the first-aid post and managed to click it back into place but the damage had been done. The injury really put paid to me for a long period of time. Three months later I was demobbed and it was time to return home and find a job again. Fortunately, they were starting to build the Felindre steelworks to the north of Swansea and I managed to get a job as a clerk in the office.

Although I had no way of knowing at the time, that fall robbed me of being part of a record in Welsh rugby that is long overdue to be broken – playing in a winning side against New Zealand! As the history books show, my team-mates went on to beat the All Blacks that December and the feat has yet to be repeated.

I could feel sorry for myself but I have accepted that it is just the way it is; in sport you sometimes get injured. There is no point beating yourself up over it, you just have to get on with it and try to get back on your feet – something I was to get more than used to!

Just before I was demobbed I was called into the CO's office and asked if I would consider making a career in the Marines. He said that I could move on to what he called an elite group of people with my fitness but there was a catch – I would have to sign up for ten years. Now the idea really appealed to me, as I loved life in the Marines, but at the end of the day ten years seemed like a lifetime and, if truth be known, I missed my mother's cooking too much, so I said no.

CHAPTER 8

Behind the
Iron Curtain

I HAD RECOVERED sufficiently to return to Swansea for pre-season training in the summer of 1954. With St Helen's being situated where it is, right on the seafront, sometimes we used to train on the beach; running around chasing a ball on lovely sunny evenings really got us fit.

On one such evening it was so warm I decided that I'd go in the sea for a swim after we'd finished training. I got undressed and, as there was nobody about except us players, I decided I'd have a naked swim. There were three or four of us splashing about but eventually I was left on my own enjoying the water. When I decided it was time to come out I discovered that they had taken my clothes. There I was, as naked as the day I was born, on Swansea beach!

The changing rooms, under the large wooden stand, were only 500 yards or so away across Oystermouth Road, and fortunately the area was tree lined. With little choice, I sort of flittered from one tree to the other. Each time someone walked by I would hide behind a tree or a bush. Eventually, I came to the players' entrance, having made a mad dash across the road. I remember waiting, looking up and down for the all clear, before I ran like hell across only to find that they had locked the bloody door! There I was, naked with my back to the road when, suddenly, along came the Mumbles bus, and it was full. I did my best to hide my face but when I looked to see the back of the bus disappearing I saw that all the people on board had rushed to one side to see this naked person.

They let me in eventually, after about ten minutes of never being so embarrassed in my life, but the damaged had been done. When I looked at the local paper, the *Evening Post*, the following day there was a story asking, 'Who was the naked rugby player spotted outside St Helen's?'

To start the season the Swansea committee had arranged a ground-breaking preseason tour that saw us become the first team to go behind the Iron Curtain, with a trip to Romania.

Incidentally, in what would be a great quiz question, our squad welcomed a guest player on the tour in the form of Carwyn James. He had yet to become a Llanelli player at that point and was invited along by Swansea who were impressed with his displays when representing the Royal Navy.

We left from Heathrow in July, travelling by Sabena Airlines and landed in Amsterdam. From there we were transferred to three wartime planes, old DC7s, which were still painted in green and brown camouflage and had been sent over from Romania to collect us. They were normally freight planes and only had enough room for eight passengers, so we needed the three. I boarded the first plane and when I got on it was just a plain floor with small armchair seats that had not been secured, so when the plane started climbing you had to hang on for dear life. There were no structures inside the fuselage except for a little cupboard for the toilet, so you could see the cockpit. The pilot couldn't speak English so he was telling us in this foreign language what he was doing while waving his arms about. He had a big, bushy beard and I can still see him now as he threw little lunch boxes at us with two sandwiches and an apple inside. Then we hit a thunderstorm and the plane, which was more or less dark inside, was suddenly lit up each time the lightning came. The pilot pointed downwards so we thought that he was going to land, but he simply reduced altitude to get out of the area of the storm and fly underneath it. It was bumpy and we were tossed about. At one point I looked through the small window during a lightning flash and, to my horror, I saw that we couldn't have been more than 100 feet above the top of the mountains. To this day that was the scariest flight I have ever endured.

We eventually came out of the storm and arrived in Bucharest. We were met by a brass band and a small welcoming party hung garlands of flowers around our necks. Many of the players were in the first plane. The committee was in the second plane, with the rest of the players in the third. We were told that the other two planes had turned back and wouldn't arrive until the morning.

We were taken down these cobbled streets to our hotel in the middle of the city. I must admit I've never seen a poorer place in my life. Everything was run-down and everyone looked so poor. I thought to myself, 'We've come to a right old place here.' We checked into our threadbare rooms and went down for the evening meal of black bread and some sort of large salami sausage. We eventually went to our rooms but we couldn't sleep. Outside the windows the streets were all cobbled and a succession of tanks – their army was moving somewhere – rattled past all night long keeping us awake. That was our welcome to Bucharest.

The rest of the contingent arrived the next day and we trained on a little green section of the city. Unfortunately Romania was basking in a heatwave, with temperatures around 100 degrees Fahrenheit and the sweat was just pouring off of us.

The next day we played against the Romanian national side in an old concrete soccer arena, with room for around 30,000 people in there. Even though the kick-off was 5 o'clock in the evening, the heat in the stadium was a tremendous 114 degrees Fahrenheit! By half-time all the players had sweat rings all around their faces but there was not a lot of water to take in, which I suspected was a ploy by the Romanian Union to weaken us.

Within ten minutes of the restart I was caught by three or four of the Romania forwards, following a short kick ahead from the scrum-half, and I was sort of herded into touch. Being a soccer stadium, space was in short supply, and there was a little wall running all the way around the pitch, about three or four feet from the touchline. I came in contact with that wall. I knew straight away that I'd suffered a bad injury because my right arm had disappeared somewhere around the back of my shoulder. It was exactly the same injury that Brian O'Driscoll received on the Lions tour of New Zealand in 2009, which is one of the worst you can get. I managed to get up but I must have resembled Quasimodo because I had this big hunchback. I was quickly bundled into a car alongside Martin Davies, one of the Swansea committee men, along with one of the Romanian representatives, and taken to hospital. I will always remember walking up to this red-bricked building, with a tower on top, and in through big glass doors. I couldn't raise my head and, as we walked down the passages, there were people lying on either side of the corridor trying to keep cool; by the looks of them they weren't long for this life. They were in very bad shape and I thought to myself, 'What have I got myself into?' It is one thing to be injured in this country but never get injured in a third world or developing country.

I was taken down to a small surgery-type room with a long settee. A doctor came in immediately but I didn't have much faith in him because he was wearing a coat which had been white about six months previously. He hadn't shaved for a couple of weeks, had big bags under his eyes and had a cigarette, half of which was ash, hanging from his mouth. He took a look at me and said something in Romanian; we had great difficulty in communicating. He signalled towards the settee, so I sat down and then lay down. The next hour was the worst period of my life as he tried all ways to get my arm back in its shoulder socket. He tugged, he pulled, he crunched – at one stage he had his knee under my arm and then his foot on top of my arm. I was sweating buckets and clearly on the verge of blacking out but I thought I had to hang on. It was a dreadful experience, that doctor was my worst nightmare. I could hear the bones crunching but, try as he might, he just couldn't get the shoulder back in. In the end he gave in and opened his heart up. He said he was sorry but he couldn't do anything for me. I thought, 'I'm really in trouble here.'

Thankfully, the Romanian representative went out, made a telephone call, and came back in. He gestured for us to follow him and we were taken back to the car and driven to the other side of Bucharest, stopping at this very tall building standing on its own. When we went through the doors I immediately knew that we were in an altogether different league of hospital; it must have been the hospital for the hierarchy of Romania. The doctor who came to see me was slim, well dressed in a dark suit and could speak English.

I was put in front of a big scanner, examined and, within two minutes, he'd put my arm back in. It was then put in plaster with my elbow sticking out at a right angle in a very awkward position altogether. And that's how I stayed for the whole tour. There was no question of being put on a plane home straight away in those days. I would have to wait for the scheduled flight at the end of the tour. It was difficult enough just getting out of bed in the mornings let alone struggling through the next ten days or so. When we eventually got back to Heathrow I must admit that it was the best place I'd ever seen. To cap it all off, a letter was waiting for me when I got home from my employers at Felindre, informing me that I had been sacked for taking time off work to tour; not the way they would treat Leigh Halfpenny today, I'm sure!

I was supposed to keep the plaster on for six weeks but, by the time I got back to Bynea, I couldn't stand it any longer. I said to my brother Len, 'Get the scissors out. And cut the bloody thing off.' And that's what he did. I was plastered from my tummy all the way up to my neck, to keep the whole thing in place, and he took a scissors to it and cut it into two halves. With a great deal of pain and difficulty, I managed to get my arm down to my side where it hung limp and useless.

I had to wait around two weeks before I could meet a specialist, by the name of Dr Gordon Rowley, and in that time I dislocated my arm several times! I would be lying in bed and I'd yawn and I'd stretch my arms and suddenly there was a click and my arm would pop out. I used to keep a small empty bottle of pop at the side of the bed and when my arm went out I had a knack of putting it underneath my armpit and then squeezing my arm back into place. I knew then that I had a major problem.

The appointment with Dr Rowley was in the old Swansea Hospital on St Helen's Road. As I was still under 21, I had to take my father with me and he hated hospitals. He had never been in one in his life and was terrified, which was not a very good start. My father's fear stemmed from when he was 15 and had a job helping to repoint the stonework on Loughor Bridge. The tide was out when one of the workmen fell and landed on the rocks and fractured his skull. They had to send for the doctor, who was in the little cottage hospital in Gorseinon, and he came by horse and cart. My father said his co-worker had a wound which was open from his forehead all the way to the back of his head, and he had to hold him down for the doctor to stitch him up.

We were shown into a room and waited for a while and then Dr Gordon Rowley came in. He was Canadian and had lost the sight of one eye in the war. When he sat down you could see there was a deficiency in that one eye and, of course, my father was horrified.

Dr Rowley said that there had been a successful operation in Australia on someone with a similar injury but he could only give me odds of 40 to 60 per cent that it would be successful in my case. He said he was prepared to do if I was prepared to take the chance.

I turned to my father and said in Welsh, knowing that Dr Rowley wouldn't follow, 'What do you think?'

He was shocked that my chances were so slim and replied, 'Listen, no one-eyed surgeon is going to take a knife to you.'

However I said, 'I'm willing to take the chance because it's no good as it is. Whatever happens afterwards, happens afterwards. If my playing career is at an end, then it's at an end.'

I told Dr Rowley I wanted to proceed and he said, because of my age, my father would have to sign a consent form before he could go any further. I passed it to my father but he refused to sign it point-blank. We were at loggerheads and I told Dr Rowley that I would take it home and convince him to sign it.

What I really did was forge my father's signature. I had to go to Penrhiwtyn Infirmary in Neath but unfortunately I had a slight cold so the operation was put back a day. They still booked me into a bed next to this chap who had fallen off scaffolding on a building site in Neath. In the middle of the night he had an epileptic fit, there was a hell of a commotion and there I was, holding this man down on the bed, with my good arm, while the nurse was sticking a spoon into his mouth. I thought, 'What a place to be!'

The operation took place on my 21st birthday, not that I knew anything about it at the time as I was out cold for nine hours. I didn't wake until the day after my birthday and when I woke I had to go to the toilet. I managed to stagger to the cubicle, which I shouldn't have done I suppose, and when I got there I looked in the mirror and saw that my face was yellow; it must have been one hell of an operation. I then discovered that they had put me in a nappy of all things. I got it off, did what I had to do, and sort of staggered back to bed feeling very, very groggy. Two days' later they took the dressings off my shoulder to have a look. When I looked down I nearly fainted. I supposed I had gone along blindly thinking an operation's an operation but when I saw the extent of it – I had 57 stitches staring me in the face – I could see the enormity of what they'd done. I later learnt that they had taken a huge flap off my shoulder to drill and plate it back together again.

I used to go down to a little gymnasium where I was shown how to do some exercises to try and get my arm moving again. The first time I was there for about half an hour and I couldn't get my arm past my hip. I didn't have the strength to raise it but I continued to struggle until the sweat poured off me and in the end the nurse said, 'You're doing too much, you've got to cool down.' But I was determined to get myself back. I gradually improved a little and a month later I was released to come home.

It must have taken me another two months before I could actually raise my arm to the height of the table, if I was sitting down, but I couldn't get the thing further than that. I used to go back and forth to St Helen's Road to the Swansea Hospital where they would stick a needle into me to knock me out in order to manipulate my arm. After the first time I came around, sitting on a chair, and they told me to hang around for 20 minutes to recover before going home. But, of course, I had a bus to catch so off I went, walking down St Helen's Road like a drunken sailor. My head was all over the place and everything was blurred but I managed to get to the bus station. It took the whole trip to Bynea before I got all my senses back. The next time I made sure I took my time and spent an hour at the hospital, having cups of tea, before I got on the bus to come home.

It was to take me nine months before I could touch my forehead. To relieve the boredom, I learned to play darts and how to write with my left hand.

I then put in for an army pension because I was still rather disabled and there was no way I was able to work. I was told to go to Carmarthen for a medical. I walked in to find three doctors sat at this table. They asked me to do certain things and, of course, I couldn't get my arm to rise above my eye level.

They then gave me a 50 per cent disability pension and suggested that I go and get a light job on a brush somewhere, sweeping floors.

You may think that I left there with my spirits in the gutter but I was never depressed by what the doctors told me – I always knew I would get there at some point or other, and that I would play again. The sports psychologists today call it a positive mental attitude. Back then it was known as strength of character, I guess.

CHAPTER 9

The Entrepreneur

SIX MONTHS AFTER the operation I was still kicking my heels and didn't have a job, so I decided to start up my own little business. I had found a small building in the village and I bought a big bench saw and an old Massey Ferguson tractor, which I used to power the saw, and I became something of a lumberjack. I wanted to get myself fit again and get my shoulder right, so I used to take a big axe and go around cutting down trees for people and sawing them up for firewood. I also provided timber for the building trade and gradually built the business up sufficiently enough to make a living.

I was really determined because I didn't want to be a failure in life. I had left school with very little education and if rugby was to be taken away from me – which I never allowed myself to think would happen – I didn't want to end up in a dead-end job pushing a broom around like those doctors had advised I do. When I approached my local bank manager for £100 to start my business, he dismissed me. Fortunately, my brothers managed to scrape the money together for me. It's something I will always be grateful for and it made me strive to be successful so I could pay them back – which I did.

As far as rugby was concerned I had to content myself with being a reluctant spectator but, when the Five Nations rolled around once more, there was a Davies from Bynea on the team sheet, my brother Len. He had been quietly making a name for himself as a tough and talented flanker for Llanelli and was rewarded with his first cap against France in the Arms Park on 27 March 1954.

It was the third game of that season and Len had been picked to bolster the side – something that worked, as Wales won by 19 points to 13. Frustratingly, however, I was unable to see him play that day because, as usual, you only had two tickets and they went to my parents. The fact that I had starred for Wales the previous season cut no ice with the WRU – can you imagine them treating their injured players like that today?

Fortunately, Len's next match, a 15–3 win against Scotland, was at St Helen's and I found myself standing amongst the masses on the big bank as the national anthem was being played. I must admit there were tears in my eyes as I looked over and saw my brother Len standing there singing away. I was very emotional that day, to think that two brothers from one family in a small village had succeeded in getting to the top of the tree. The only downside was that I wasn't out there with him.

Len was again selected to play for Wales the following season and, as I was still not fully recovered from my shoulder injury, I resumed my role as my brother's number one fan.

The first game of the championships was in Cardiff against Ireland and that's where I first saw Tony O'Reilly. He was playing centre that day and I remember one furious clash between Len and O'Reilly where the Irish centre found himself flat on the floor gasping for breath; I would often remind him about that when we later became good friends.

I had travelled to watch the game with a crowd from the village on the local Eynon's Buses which were never in danger of picking up a speeding ticket! After the game the driver would wait for you to have your drink and then we would crawl home at around 30mph. Then we would be stuck at the level crossing in Port Talbot for about half an hour waiting for the train to come through. It used to take you at least three hours to come back from Cardiff in those days.

I will never forget the return journey that day. As the bus

was chugging up a hill, doing about 10 mph, there was a very drunken chap on board dancing about. Now he must have been about 17 stone and he was stomping in the aisle when he suddenly went through the floorboards. His legs were going like mad to keeping up with the bus. He was eventually dragged to safety but it was like watching Fred Flintstone!

Sadly, following the Irish game, Len became unwell and was unable to complete the season but he had done enough to be short-listed for the 1955 Lions tour to South Africa. Although we never knew it at the time, Len would never play rugby for his country again.

I had already been asked if I was available, but my injuries prevented me from taking part. I have always thought how marvellous it would have been if we were the first two brothers to have played for the Lions together; it would have been great.

I continued to throw myself into my work and, around nine months after I'd had the operation, I was cutting down a tree, which of course I had to climb to lop it off, and I fell. I must have fallen about fifteen feet and landed on my right shoulder, which was the one that had been operated on. Lo and behold nothing happened. I came out of it with a couple of bruises but the shoulder was much eased. I thought, 'OK, if I can fall off a tree, I can play again.'

I was to get my chance four months' later when the British and Irish Lions came back from South Africa where they'd had a successful tour, drawing the Test series. For one reason or another, the Lions had arranged an end-of-season game against Llanelli and they must have been short at that time because their star outside-half, Cliff Morgan, phoned me up and asked if I was fit? I didn't hesitate and said yes. After all, in all likelihood I would have been selected for the tour, had I been fit.

I had built myself up to be quite a strong young man by that time and I left Stradey Park that evening having injured quite a few Llanelli players in a fierce game. One Llanelli centre had to have hospital treatment after one of my tackles.

I don't know what I was thinking but my playing that game came to the notice of Swansea and the WRU. I was also given an almighty row by my surgeon Dr Gordon Rowley, as he hadn't given me permission to play again. I acted naïve and said that I didn't know I needed permission. He was very cross but he must have been quietly proud that his operation, the first of its kind in this country, had been a huge success. Looking back, I also think that my will-power and sheer bloody-minded determination played a big part in my recovery. You can have all the medical treatment and rehabilitation in the world – as players have in abundance today – but at the end of the day, you should never underestimate the power of the mind.

The next season I wanted to ease myself gently back into playing and I thought that my village team was the best place to do so. I asked Swansea if they would release me for the period up to Christmas but they refused point-blank. They said that I should be playing for their second XV or Mumbles or somebody in that area. This didn't appeal to me and I dug my heels in. The situation was inflamed by the fact that Swansea hadn't taken much notice of me when I was having my operation; no-one came to see me and I think that they believed that I was finished with rugby. Suddenly, now that I was playing again, they wanted me to come back.

It reached a bit of a stalemate. I think they were a bit afraid that I would go to Llanelli, but that wasn't the case. I just wanted to play for Bynea to get myself back into the game. It would also have been a help to the village and I would be playing with my old pals again. Suddenly, it got worse and Swansea stopped me playing entirely. They refused my transfer request, so I threatened that I would play soccer instead. Thankfully, the WRU stepped in and said, 'Let him go back to the village.' And that's what I did.

Of course, it soured my relationship with Swansea. I did

promise that I would play one of their games over Christmas, which I did, but I wasn't totally fit and I had an indifferent game. In the clubhouse later I was having a quiet little drink and I overheard one of the committee men standing behind me talking to some of the reporters. Whether he knew I was in earshot I don't know, but the committee man said, 'I think Davies has had it. I don't think we need him any more. It's obvious that he's not going to be much good.'

If I had been a little bolder I would have taken him to task but I wasn't and I thought to myself, 'That's it; cheerio Swansea.' And I went back to play for my village.

Fortunately, my relationship with the WRU, especially the Big Five, was a very good one and they stuck with me all the way, even to the extent that they picked me for the first Welsh trial, which was in Caerphilly. The village of Bynea emptied and three bus loads went up to give their support to the local boy. I had a reasonable game which meant that they picked me for the second trial which was in Swansea.

Reading the programme before the game made me smile. You had a list of players from Cardiff, Aberavon, Llanelli, Swansea and Newport and there, at the very top of them, was a player from little old Bynea! I thought that was great. I had a very good game in Swansea, it was very impressive, and the Big Five said to me, 'We like the look of you and we want to select you but you've got to go back and play for either Swansea or Llanelli.'

Now Bynea at the time were on a great run and we'd reached the quarter-finals of the West Wales Cup. It was a big deal for Bynea and I couldn't let them down so I said, 'Not yet.'

Despite my decision, I was picked for the final trial in Cardiff. I thought to myself, 'If I outplay the other fullback this will be a real *Roy of the Rovers* story.' I had a chance here of a player from a small village club being chosen to play for his country at Twickenham.

Unfortunately, it wasn't the case. I think the WRU chickened out a bit and the other fullback, Garfield Owen, was picked and that was that. Of course, we were then knocked out of the cup in the semi-final.

CHAPTER 10

A Llanelli player at long last

THE FOLLOWING SEASON I finally made the move to my home town club. My first game for the Scarlets was away to Bath and, while it was nice to finally pull on a Llanelli shirt, the best thing about it was being back in first-class rugby. Our captain that day was a chap called Peter Evans who had a dreadful stutter. To offset his stutter he used to issue little notes to players with the tactics written down. It was quite bizarre really. There we would be, sat in the changing room before the game with these little notes in front of us saying what we had to do, but, of course, with his stutter being so dreadful there was no way he could have given us a team talk.

The game started well for us and we were pressing on the Bath 25-yard line when the ball went back to their fullback and he put in a long kick which went all the way down to our 25-yard line.

Suddenly, I heard Peter shouting, 'Du der du du doo, du der du du doo!' and suddenly everybody was rushing back to defend.

Now I hadn't heard that before, so after the game I said to Peter, 'What does this du der du du doo mean?'

He replied, 'Listen g-g-g-good boy, I s-s-s-should have b-b-b-been sh-sh-sh-shouting, s-s-s-sound the retreat b-b-b-but b-b-b-by the time I got that out they w-w-w-would h-h-h-have s-s-s-scored t-t-t-twice!'

The first derby game against my former club was at St

Helen's and I suppose it was a bit of a grudge match. I was playing centre, with Carwyn James at outside-half, and within ten minutes I had gone over for a try and then I made two tries for Llanelli; the flanker and the winger. It was a good feeling walking off knowing I had helped win the game. As far as I was concerned, when you have someone saying that you are no good it's a case of saying, 'Well, take that!'

One thing I can say about the derbies between the Jacks and the Turks is that I never lost a game against Swansea when I played for Llanelli. They were tough games and they were tight games but we won them all, which was great for the town. D C Williams, the then manager of Trostre works, used to say, 'When Llanelli beat Swansea, the following Monday our production is sky-high!'

I learned quite a lot from my time with Swansea and not just on the field. They were a group of middle-class players, whereas Llanelli were more industrial working class. Now I'm not saying we were thugs but, being from a working-class background, as I was myself, we were tougher. I knew I had made the correct decision and there was no fondness, at that time, for Swansea in my book. To demonstrate this there is one incident on another occasion when we visited Swansea for an evening game. In the home side was the north Walian Dewi Bebb, who was a brilliant wing and very quick. He had come down to study at Carmarthen's Trinity College and Swansea picked him up and he soon went on to play for Wales.

The first half was a very tight and fractious game, as the derby games always were, and the crowd wasn't very pleasant at times, showing its anger by stamping on the wooden floor of the large stand. Just before half-time Swansea had the ball on their own 25 and they moved it left across towards the stand area, where it came to Dewi Bebb. He shot down the line like a rocket. As I was sort of lazing about at the back, I thought I had better go and have a look at what was happening because there could be a little bit of danger here. As I was running across the field I saw the amazing sight of Dewi Bebb flying down the wing with the crowd in the background all getting on their feet in excitement – it was like a Mexican wave. He kept on going and suddenly I confronted him. I knew he had a terrific sidestep off his left foot, so I pretended to move into an area that would lead him to step me. Unfortunately for him, he took the bait and came off his left foot and I caught him with a tremendous tackle that flattened him. As he lay on the ground the referee blew up and I thought, 'I've done some damage here.'

The Swansea trainer came on and he looked daggers at me because Dewi was still out. He had to give him more than the obligatory two dabs of the magic sponge. You were only allowed two because the trainer would have to go all the way back into the dressing room and refill his sponge bag before he could use it again!

After a few minutes the trainer managed to get Dewi on his feet again but he was puffing madly and I thought I had better go over and see if he was OK. As I walked over there were some boos from the crowd of course because he was a favourite.

As we were both Welsh speakers I asked him in Welsh, 'Are you all right?'

He looked at me with these wild eyes and said, 'I thought we were friends?!'

I replied. 'Well we were friends yesterday, and we'll probably be friends tomorrow, but we're not bloody friends today.' I pointed to my jersey and put his hand on his and I said, 'Look at the different colours.'

Of course, being a north Walian he didn't quite understand the rivalry of the scarlet of Llanelli and the white of the Swansea Jacks but he had been given a crash course that night!

On the field that season the team was coming together nicely and we had a large number of players, such as R H

Williams, Carwyn James, Ray Williams and Cyril Davies, who were either internationals or internationals in the making.

One of the stars was undoubtedly Carwyn James and of course he went on to become one of the great coaches of any generation but, strangely, when we were playing together he didn't show any tendency towards that side of the game.

The other thing about Carwyn that I will always remember was that he hated playing against Aberavon. That was down to two hard flankers, Rory O'Connor and Peter Jones, the father of Lyn Jones, the former Neath and Llanelli flanker who went on to coach the Ospreys and Dragons. He would try everything to avoid the Talbot Athletic ground, saying the place was dangerous.

But that season the Wizards didn't stop us and we had a run of 13 victories without a loss and the side developed a huge team spirit which counted for a lot and made up for the lack of facilities.

When I look at today's players with their purpose-built training facilities, including indoor pitches, I catch myself laughing. The changing rooms in the old Stradey were sparse to say the least. We were all crammed into a small room, with only around 18 inches of personal space with one little hook to put all your clothes on. After games all the committee used to crowd into the changing room, and, if it had been a wet afternoon, by the time you came in to get changed, you would find your nice, clean white shirt on the floor with large footprints on it.

They had an old bath, which had been installed in the 1920s, probably by hobblers from the old steelworks. It had an 18-inch high wall of concrete all the way round, which would be full of dirty tepid water. You would just about fit 15 players in like sardines. If you won the game you would get some of the bigger forwards standing on top of the wall and jumping in. If you were already in, you would be swept along by the wave and, as the floor was concrete, when you got out there would be no skin left on your bum.

Now the chap who used to clean the changing rooms was called Elvet Rees. He always had a little cigarette in the corner of his mouth and a cap pulled tight to his head. He used to lean on his brush waiting for us to change so that he could sweep up. He heard me complaining one day and suddenly, out of the blue, Elvet spoke up, 'Hey, listen good boy, Albert Jenkins bathed in that bath and if it was good enough for Albert, it's bloody good enough for you.'

That brought me down a peg or two because nobody could play better than Albert. He was an icon. It was said that the children of Llanelli knew about Albert before they knew about the royal family.

On the subject of the old concrete bath, the thing to do was to get in there first, before all the big lads would jump in, and you would then get a bit of space and clean water. But, on occasions, you would be caught out and everybody would land in the bath together. Some of the front row boys were in a world of their own and played a totally different game to everybody else. When they didn't have enough room, one of them would pee in the air, a six-foot jet stream, and suddenly there was plenty of room in there!

Of course, Howard Ash, one of our props and a hell of a character, would just gulp some water in and spout it out in defiance.

Conditions were quite poor all round. When it came to training on dark winter evenings we only had the one floodlight on the main pitch. It was fixed onto the solitary stand, which incidentally was a popular spot for youngsters in the town to do their courting – they used to say more people in Llanelli were conceived in that stand than actually went to watch the team play!

Training beneath that solitary spotlight certainly made things interesting. Now Wyn Evans, who was our captain for a season or two, would often arrive late and, being a chain-smoker, he would set off on a few laps of the field to warm up and all you would see was the red glow of his cigarette circling around in the dark!

During games there was always great banter from the crowd on the Tanner Bank and you would often hear some wise-cracking loud voice coming over. Once I missed a kick – it hit the crossbar and came back in front of goal – and this huge voice came out of the Tanner Bank and said, 'Good God boy, you couldn't kick a fart!' It was all part of the fun.

One of my favourites was uttered in a charity game that was arranged in the aftermath of the mountain moving in Godre'r-graig, in the Swansea Valley – it had moved 12 inches in a year and it was now threatening a row of 20 cottages.

The late Brian Thomas, the second row from Neath, a huge character, was playing. The move had gone to the old stand side of Stradey and suddenly Brian had lost a boot. The move then went up to the Tanner Bank, where the ball was kicked into touch. A lineout was formed and everyone was waiting for Brian to arrive. He quietly put his boot back on and, instead of running to join the lineout, he walked. He plodded and he plodded across the field.

Suddenly this voice cried out, 'Come on Brian bach, the mountain is moving quicker than you!'

Besides playing all the top Welsh teams, we had regular fixtures against the best of the English sides. One of the highlights used to be the trip up to Leicester. Usually we would have a very good driver with Eynon's Buses and he was quite quick. Unfortunately, on one occasion, he was ill and they brought in the driver who used to do the Llanelli/Carmarthen run. He wasn't very good at all and did 30 mph all the way up. Every queue he came to he would put his foot on the brake, it was like kangaroo petrol, and it took us ten hours to get to Leicester.

We finally arrived at the Bell Hotel in Leicester, two hours overdue, and went straight to bed.

The next day everyone got together and onto the bus at 12 o'clock. The driver drove us to the ground but, of course, he couldn't find a place to park. So, after dropping us off, the police guided him half a mile away and then brought him back, which was very kind of them.

Now he was a very small chap, I can see him now, with his flat cap on sideways. We played the game, I'm not sure if we won or lost, maybe because there was a free bar after the game. This little driver was sat on a stool next to the bar. I don't suppose he had ever had a free bar in his life because 7 o'clock came and there was a hell of a thud. He had fallen off his stool because he was completely legless. He needed a taxi to get back to the hotel.

The players eventually made it back at around 11 o'clock. There was a small room, on the hotel's second floor, where you could have a few drinks. We went in and made ourselves at home and there were the usual high jinks. Now, there was a policeman outside, walking back and forth in front of the hotel. One of our notorious front-row forwards peed on him through the window. There was quite a kerfuffle and about ten minutes later his sergeant and another three policemen arrived in the room.

The sergeant said to the policeman, who looked as though he had been in a shower of rain, 'Do you recognise a face?'

He replied, 'No, I didn't see his face.'

So the sergeant said to all 15 players, who were standing in a line, 'Strip off, we'll have an identity parade.'

We were halfway to stripping – it was getting serious – when Handel Rogers, our chairman, stepped in and said, 'You can't do that.'

Luckily it ended there with a general apology. I had never before been involved in an identity parade, especially one that didn't include the face!

The little driver had a hell of a hangover the next morning and we were supposed to leave for home at 10 o'clock but he couldn't find the bus. We looked everywhere but couldn't find it. He had forgotten where he had put it. We had to have the police out to look for it. It was eventually found at 12 o'clock and we didn't get home until 3 o'clock in the morning.

With even relatively small clubs these days enjoying tours to places such as Australia and Florida, life was far from as glamorous in my day and my first tour with Llanelli took me back behind the Iron Curtain all the way to Mother Russia at the height of the Cold War!

It was 1957 and I believe we were the first Welsh team to travel to Russia to take part in the third World Youth Games. It was a most unusual journey of around 2,000 miles over five days which saw us make our way down to Dover, before catching the ferry across to Ostend, then travel to Berlin where we crossed over to communist East Germany through Checkpoint Charlie. From there the train to Moscow was packed with Red Army personnel, who viewed our exuberance and freedom with great suspicion. We enjoyed the odd sing-song and our high spirits were probably something they hadn't seen before. The only food supplied to us was a fat German sausage with some black loaves of bread – I starved for two days.

It was quite an experience passing through the old Iron Curtain at that time. We got to Moscow and were welcomed by young girls with garlands of flowers which were draped around our necks. We were stationed just off Red Square in a building belonging to the state university with a giant red star stuck on top of it.

The next morning we strolled across the bridge into Red Square itself, which was a very large cobbled area. We queued for about half an hour to go and visit the tombs of Lenin and Stalin. We were eventually ushered in and there were these two huge glass cases. A very yellow looking Lenin lay in one

Romanian Whites! The Swansea side before setting off to sample the delights of Romania. I'm in the middle row and so new I haven't even earned my club blazer! In the back row, fifth from the left, is a certain Carwyn James.
© South Wales Evening Post

Clearing our lines: in action for Wales at St Helen's ground in Swansea with Haydn Morgan in the background.
© Trinity Mirror

In from the back: just about to receive a pass from Cliff Morgan (who is outside Llanelli wing Jeff Howells) in a game in Cardiff against England.

Anthem: Wales lining up against France in Stade Colombes, 1953. From left to right: Ken Jones, Alun Thomas, John Gwilliam, Rees Stephens, Roy John, Cliff Morgan, Gareth Griffiths, Sid Judd, Terry Davies, John Robbins, Billy Williams, Clem Thomas, D M Davies, Trevor Lloyd, and our captain that day, Bleddyn Williams.

Brothers in red: myself and Len wearing our caps which came a year after one another.

Russian rendezvous: this photograph was taken at 6.30am on Llanelli station waiting for a train to start our Russian adventure.

© South Wales Evening Post

Russian return: Llanelli president Handel Rogers, his grandson, Ray Williams, and yours truly shortly after arriving home safely in Llanelli from our Russian adventure.

© South Wales Evening Post

Terry the Barbarian: looking dapper in my Barbarians' blazer in 1957 while on a tour of Canada, and meeting a gentleman originally from Llanelli.

Super six! The Llanelli players picked to play for Wales against Australia in 1958. Back row: Ray Williams, Cyril Davies, Wynne Evans; sitting: Carwyn James, club president Handel Rogers, and R H Williams; with myself cross-legged on the floor.

Poster boy: yours truly wearing his British and Irish Lions tie and blazer for the tour of Australia and New Zealand in 1959.

Pride of Lions: the 1959 British and Irish Lions touring party. I'm furthest right, fourth row up from the front.

Jersey boy: a spot of reminiscing over Test jerseys from the 1959 tour of Australia and New Zealand.

© *South Wales Evening Post*

Good company: attending a line-up of former Welsh captains sometime in the late 1970s. I'm in the back row, fifth from left.

Remembering Stradey. From left to right: Derek Quinnell, Phil Bennett, Doug Williams, Peter Rees and myself with a piece of artwork, unveiled in Sandy Water Park, to commemorate Stradey Park as part of the heritage trail.

© South Wales Evening Post

Name check: checking for my name on the honours' board at Parc y Scarlets.

© South Wales Evening Post

Bardic buddies! From left to right: myself, Clive Rowlands, Ray Gravell and Delme Thomas at the National Eisteddfod in Llanelli in 2000.

My best match ever! With Gillian on our wedding day, 28 September 1961.

Wedding line-up: the family photograph outside St David's church in Carmarthen. My father, Edwin, is second from the left and my mother, Alvera, next to him.

Best Bynea pals. From left to right: Des Bowen, my brother Roy, myself as the nervous groom, and Ken Lloyd.

Team Davies – with our children. From left to right: Mathew, Nicola and Richard, on my 80th birthday in 2012.

Decorated: with Gillian after collecting my MBE in 2013.

Pen pals! With my biographer Geraint Thomas at the unveiling of the old Stradey Park goal posts which have been placed on a roundabout at the eastern gateway to Llanelli.

© South Wales Evening Post

Captured on canvas: Andrew Vicari in his studio putting the finishing touches to his Terry Davies masterpiece!

Bynea boy: the portrait of me in my village colours on my wall at home.

case and then we were ushered around to see Stalin lying in state in the other. You were not allowed to speak and there were military people there guarding the whole thing with their rifles. After only a few minutes we were quickly ushered out again.

We then crossed over to the other side of the square where the famous GUM store was. This was a replica of Selfridges, apparently, and we went inside but there was virtually nothing there. It was very ornate but all the merchandise was rubbish. The only thing I bought was a Russian teddy bear for my youngest sister, Denise, who still cherishes it to this day.

The eating arrangements at the university saw us sat in a huge marquee. The food was reasonable, I must admit, and served on 50 or so long trestle tables, where all the countries sat. Next to us was the Czechoslovakian running team, complete with the great distance runner Emil Zátopek, who always had a smile on his face.

On the other side was the Oxford and Cambridge combined rowing eight, immaculately dressed in light blue and dark blue blazers, white trousers and blue cravats. They were looking like true English gentlemen. One of our hookers was Geraint Stephens from Llandybie. Now Geraint had been in the Paras and was quite a stocky chap, always with his shirt open with this great big medal depicting a paratrooper on his chest, to show everybody that he was a paratrooper. And he was quite a character with a big belly laugh.

He took a shine to the combined rowing team. Unfortunately, the day before they had capsized their boat and were feeling very embarrassed by it all. Of course, Geraint came past and muttered out of the corner of his mouth, 'Are you swimming today, boys?'

Well, you could have cut the atmosphere with a knife, everything went cold. Then he spotted that the rowing boys had all found the caviar pot and, of course, they had lashings of it on their toast. Geraint looked at it and his eyes lit up, and he said, 'Der, boys, where did you get the blackberry jam from?'

After that there was huge hilarity. From then on he was always welcomed to breakfast by the rowing crew with, 'Good morning Mr Blackberry Jam Man!'

Carwyn James was our outside-half on the Moscow trip and he was a prince on and off the field of play. Now Carwyn was a big favourite with our hosts because, being an intellectual, he had actually learned to speak Russian during his National Service as he was part of some Royal Naval intelligence unit or something.

We had been assigned a lovely interpreter who wanted to know all about Great Britain; his questions were endless. This young lad couldn't get over the freedom of our speaking and living. We would be singing on the bus and he was under the impression that all athletes should take everything seriously and this was an eye-opener to him. He had this little microphone on the bus and he pointed out all the places of note and really seemed to be enjoying himself. He sat next to Carwyn, who being a great teacher, used to correct him on a number of things.

He also learnt some things from Howard Ash! Now Howard took him under his wing a bit and he used to ask Howard the odd question. On one occasion we were sharing the bus with some female swimmers when suddenly our interpreter remembered something and he looked down at Howard and said, 'Excuse me Mr Ash, you know the word that you're always using? I've looked in my English dictionary all night and I can't find it. Could you tell me what is the meaning of this word fuck?'

The bus erupted in huge laughter and Howard stood up and mimed the meaning of the word and the young lad was so embarrassed we didn't see him for two days!

As for the rugby, our first game was against Yugoslavia – we had an easy passage in that one because we were far too good for them and won 35 points to 9, but the spies from the Romanian Rugby Union were there, thick and heavy, to have a look over us and they came up with some dirty tactics.

For a start, they changed the ball! Against Yugoslavia we were playing with a Gilbert-type ball and I kicked quite a few goals that day from quite long distances. But, when it came to the next game, the Romanians changed it to one with far more air in it than should have been, which made it difficult to kick.

The game itself was a thoroughly vicious affair – I hadn't been in such an unruly game in my life. Anything went! The referee for that game was a small Frenchman, immaculately dressed in black shorts and socks all the way up to his knees, and a black beret on his head. He couldn't speak Romanian and he couldn't speak English. We had 14 Welsh-speaking players in our side, so you can understand how the problems arose.

The first scrum went down and the big Romanian prop, opposite Howard Ash, who had his sleeves rolled up all the way to his armpits, tried to stifle our front row, but Howard reached over and bit him on the bicep. There was a commotion, and the scrum broke up and this Romanian grabbed the referee and dragged him towards Howard, who had a little smile on his face. The Romanian began gesticulating that he had been bitten by Howard – you could see a mark on his arm. Howard looked at the mark and turned and declared to the little referee, 'Those are not Welsh teeth marks.'

The game disintegrated from there and the little French referee decided enough was enough: there were bodies all over the place, so he blew his whistle and disappeared into the stand. Both teams stood around for about ten minutes until he was persuaded to return! It didn't get any better and when we had a penalty given to us on our 25, I said to Rhys Williams, who was the captain, 'What do you want to do with it?'

'Put the bloody thing up as high as you can,' he said, 'we'll storm them!'

The ball went up about 80 feet in the air and I think that all the team landed on the Romanian side. That was the last straw and the referee blew the whistle and the game finished about 20 minutes early. The result was a 6-all draw but Carwyn James had a perfectly good drop goal disallowed.

The administrators held talks and it was suggested that the game be replayed. We held a meeting with all the players and our chairman, Handel Rogers, asked, 'Hands up who wants to play the game again?' Fourteen hands went up, with the only dissenter being Cyril Davies, our centre, who said, 'I don't think we should play them again because they're cheaters. And I don't like cheaters.'

Cyril Davies was something else. He had been brought up by his two aunts who once knitted him two Llanelli socks – a left foot sock and a right sock! I had never seen that before. He also carried three pairs of boots in his bag and he would toss up which pair to wear in a particular game because he assumed they would be the lucky ones. He behaved exactly the same in a Welsh jersey. Once, we were all ready to go out against Ireland when he threw a wobbly and said he wasn't going out until Bill Clements, then the secretary of the WRU, had paid him his full expenses. He explained the secretary had not reimbursed him the correct bus fare from Ammanford to Swansea train station!

The game was eventually replayed at the end of the tour but we lost 6–3 as there was not a lot left in the tank by then. The Russian newspapers, somewhat unfairly, slated us with one report saying the Welsh players were more interested in vodka and caviar than playing rugby!

Once all the games were finished we were waiting to go home. Everyone was getting ready and the Russian authorities would say, 'You leave tomorrow.' But when tomorrow came it was the next day, all over again.

Being rugby players we decided to have a few drinks in our dormitory. The local brew was called Leningrad Beer. It was thick and dark and had a hell of a kick to it, and after two pints you didn't know where the hell you were. Things began to get rowdy and somebody threw a mattress out of a window; we were four floors up. There were a few giggles before a few minutes later a line of soldiers marched down the corridor, fully armed. They took all the mattresses off our beds and we ended up sleeping on the springs that night. It did the trick though, as the next day we were informed we were to fly out of Moscow.

We held a little leaving party with our hosts before we left in one of the university's rooms. Being a side full of Welsh speakers, we were having a good old sing-song with all the Welsh classics coming out. We took it in turns to do a solo and the last one to sing was Carwyn. I had never heard him sing before and didn't know what to expect but when he started the room fell silent. He delivered a faultless rendition of 'Myfanwy', without any music, perfectly in pitch and tune – there wasn't a dry eye in the room. That's a memory I will always treasure of Carwyn James.

Our interpreter came to wish us goodbye and I will always remember the tears streaming down his face. I doubt if he had ever enjoyed himself as much in his poor little life. The Russian tour had been a huge learning experience because you realised just how well off we were coming from this country.

I suppose by this time I was well on my way to becoming famous – in the sporting world at least. It wasn't like today, when you have any number of supposed celebrities thanks to television and the tabloids. Back then, television was for the rich and for the working man sport was the greatest form of entertainment – you only have to look at the crowds that used to flock to the sports grounds.

I first really noticed it soon after winning my first cap when my father and I attended the funeral of a cousin of my grandmother's in a place called Nantyglo. We caught a train on a November day from Llanelli and we got off at Neath and took what they called 'the little train' up to the Valleys. It was a dreary old day, with this smoky dampish atmosphere as we walked up to a council estate which was on top of the hill where they lived. My father and I had a cup of tea before the funeral and then we walked all the way down to the churchyard. We were walking behind the coffin bearers and I was speaking to one of my cousins when I caught sight of quite a crowd waiting.

I said to my cousin, 'Your father was quite a popular man judging by all these people coming out to see him off.'

He turned to me and said, 'They haven't come to see him; they heard that you were coming and they turned out for you.'

I knew then that playing for Wales must have meant something.

By then I was getting used to strangers approaching me in the street, asking for my autograph, but I must say I was completely taken aback when I was approached by a young man, as I made my way out of the players' entrance following a game down Stradey Park one evening, with a strange request.

This young chap said, 'Are you Terry Davies?'

'Yes,' I said, somewhat cautiously.

'I would like to paint you,' he said. It turned out that he was a promising artist having recently come out of the Slade School of Fine Art in London. We had a chat and eventually I agreed but we quarrelled over which jersey I would wear. He wanted me in the red of Wales but I was anxious to show my roots and wanted to wear the strip of my home village club, Bynea. That was an argument I won. I told him if, in years to come, he became famous it wouldn't matter.

His name was Andrew Vicari and he became very famous! I still have to pinch myself today when I look up at the massive six foot by four foot portrait of myself towering over our dining table, the likes of which people have paid hundreds of thousands of pounds for. For years the painting was on show in the Welsh Office in Cardiff but Andrew, who has become a close friend of mine, eventually got it back and presented it to me.

Towards the end of that season I suffered another shoulder injury, which was a broken clavicle on my left side, and once again my stop-start career was put on hold for another month or so. We were playing against Aberavon at the Talbot Athletic ground when I lined up a large forward who was on the rampage and, for once, came off second best. I didn't realise how serious it was until the following morning and, after an uncomfortable night unable to sleep, I went to hospital. I suppose Carwyn James was right... Aberavon was a dangerous place to play!

CHAPTER 11

Back from the Dead

THE 1957/58 SEASON was when my comeback was fully realised and I was once again selected to play for Wales. It really was a momentous occasion for me because from being a real no-hoper, here I was back again, like a bad penny.

The Welsh team was always announced on a Tuesday on the BBC news. I can recall sitting around the wireless with my family. We were all holding our breath, listening with great anticipation when the first name out was Terry Davies, fullback. What a feeling that was! To have overcome all my injuries after being written off by doctors, it was a sweet feeling. To have come out the other side to be selected once more was almost better than winning my first cap – it was certainly harder.

If I needed any confirmation, the newspaper headlines next day provided it, saying:

Davies back from the dead.

Another, full-page article, outlined my 'storybook comeback' following four 'calamitous years' in the injury wilderness before my 'grit and pluck, coupled with the surgeon's skill, saw a return to the national side'.

That first game back came on Saturday, 18 January 1958, against England at Twickenham. We travelled up on the Thursday and had a run out on Twickenham the next day which went quite well. However, when I woke on the Saturday, there was a hell of a gale-force wind blowing. I knew it was going to be a bad day because, back then, part of Twickenham was open to the elements. The wind would howl down making kicking difficult; it would look as if the ball was going straight through the posts but then, at the last minute, the wind would swirl and you would probably be wide by about ten yards.

England were a very strong side and very few people had much confidence in us going there and winning – one bookmaker had us down as 1/6 no-hopers. Our captain that day was Clem Thomas and, having won the toss, he chose to play with the wind in the first half.

We managed to hold our own for around 30 minutes and keep our line intact before being awarded a penalty about three yards out from the touchline and between the ten-yard line and halfway. Now, back then it was almost unheard of for someone to even try a kick from that distance, let alone put it over, as the balls were made out of leather and were much heavier, but we needed to take any opportunity to score that came along. I lined it up and, with the strong wind at my back, I kicked the goal. Suddenly we were in the lead. I suppose you could say it was a similar moment to when Gavin Henson put over another long-distance kick against the old enemy on the way to the Grand Slam in 2005. England reacted to going behind and attacked furiously, but our pack got stuck in and we managed to keep them out and reach half-time still in the lead by three points to nil.

We started the second half playing into that dreadful wind which was howling down the field. Before long their winger, Peter Thompson, managed to scuffle over in the corner to level the scores. Tries were worth three points back then. The longer the game went on, the more dispirited the English became because they weren't getting things together. You can blame the wind but it really was a battle between the two packs.

Their main threat was their backline but we managed to keep them out of the game. I remember on one occasion Jeff Butterfield, who was a great English centre, broke through and when I confronted him he only had to pass the ball to his wing for them to score. So I did the usual trick of pretending to put my arm out and move slightly towards the wing, to give him the impression that the dummy was in place, and when the dummy came I hit him with one hell of a bang and the try was saved.

With about ten minutes to go we managed to get into their half for the first time since the restart. We had been really up against it when we were awarded a penalty practically on the halfway line.

Now there was this gale-force wind blowing and Clem Thomas said to me, 'What do you think?'

I said, 'I'll never kick it in this gale.'

'Go on,' he said, 'it's the first time we've been in this half; it might be the last chance we get.'

So I thought, 'OK.' I put the ball down on the halfway line and it was virtually in the middle of the field so I had to aim at the right hand post where the wind was swirling. I shut my eyes and gave it some welly. I hung my body slightly over it to keep it low and off it went like an Exocet missile. It cut through the wind and was going straight through the posts when suddenly, at the last split-second, there was a change of wind direction, and it blew the ball against the upright. The whole stadium seemed to hold its breath and watched as the ball came back onto the crossbar and bounced up before the bloody wind blew it back infield. Now, had that kick gone over it would have won the game for us, ending a dismal run of defeats at Twickenham. However, when we took stock, we were quite pleased because everybody had written us off, yet here we were, the underdogs, managing to hold them to a draw.

The post-match dinner was held at the Mayfair Hotel in those days and we had a most enjoyable evening. My brother Roy and his friend had come up to see the game and I managed to meet up with them briefly for a drink when he said, 'Why don't you come back with us in the car in the morning?'

I thought that would make a nice change and be a lot quicker, so I approached Eric Evans, the Secretary of the WRU, to ask permission. He was so thrilled by the drawn game that he said, 'Yes, anything for you Davies!'

I was collected from the hotel at 9 o'clock the next morning for the drive home. It was one hell of a long journey but not as long as it would be on the train because in those days there was always rail workings on a Sunday, where you would be stopped and shown around various detours and arrive back at Paddington where you started from! It was not unknown to leave Paddington at around 9 o'clock in the morning and it would be about quarter to five or thereabouts before you arrived home in Llanelli. But, looking back, it would have been better had I taken the train that day.

Now the M4 didn't exist in 1958 and we came back along the old road system which, including the Oxford bypass, was quite a journey. We had been sitting in this car for three hours and were driving down through the Cotswolds when we saw a little café and, as it was approaching lunch time, I suggested we stop for a cup of tea and something to eat.

Roy found a spot in the car park and we walked inside and sat down. There were a lot of Welsh supporters heading back home and the place was pretty full. As we waited for our food to arrive, I noticed three boys in the corner of the café looking over to me. It was the usual thing and you had to sort of put up with the fact that everybody knew who you were and wanted to talk to you. I suppose it must have been a bit of a surprise for them to see me there.

Then one of them got up and came over to our table. He said, 'You're Terry Davies, aren't you?'

I nodded my head and said, 'Yes.'

He said, 'Great game yesterday. Do you mind autographing something for us?'

'Of course,' I said thinking, 'here we go again.'

'Right,' he said, 'I'll go and get it.' Out he went and the next thing I saw was him lugging this five-foot-long piece of four-by-two, which was painted white.

Now I'd been asked before to sign the back of cigarette packets, programmes, shirts, you name it, whatever was available, but I thought to myself, 'This is rather unusual.'

He placed the piece of timber on the table and I could see there was a little hook on one end and it suddenly occurred to me that it was a section of somebody's crossbar.

I asked him, 'Where did you get this from?'

He replied, 'I'll tell you in a minute if you can sign it in three places.' He was a short, stocky bloke and, as I signed it, I asked, 'Where are you from then, boys?'

'Tenby,' one of them replied.

Having finished signing the piece of wood I handed the pen back and the first guy said, 'Right, thank you. Now I will tell you. This is the crossbar that you kicked the ball against yesterday. We snook into Twickenham last night and cut it down.'

'Oh God!' I thought. 'If this gets out, I'm in trouble.' I immediately saw the prospects of me being dropped by the WRU and on any future tours I would be ostracized.

I was very quiet for the rest of that journey. Thankfully, by the time we arrived home, at around about 4 o'clock, nothing had been on the radio news about a stolen crossbar from the sacred home of rugby, so I thought I was in the clear.

The next morning I went down to my sawmill and was busy cutting some timber up when David Nicholas, the Secretary of Bynea Rugby Club, came rushing in. Now David was quite an excitable chap, always rushing back and forth, so I didn't think much of it. Then he asked, 'Have you seen the newspapers? You're in trouble, you've signed something. They've cut the crossbar down at Twickenham and there's hell to play. I've had a phone call from Eric Evans, the Secretary of the WRU, and he wants you to phone him immediately.'

I turned the saw off and went to find a telephone. I was

connected to the WRU and I asked, 'What's the problem, Mr Evans?' It was always Mr Evans, as he was the man with the expenses so you always had to be polite to him.

He said, 'What the hell have you been up to Davies?!'

'Pardon?' I said.

'What have you been up to?' he repeated.

I said, 'I haven't been up to anything.'

'Well,' he said, 'you've signed that bloody crossbar and the English Union are playing hell with us.'

'Well,' I said, 'I'm sorry but I didn't know it was the crossbar when I signed it.' I explained to him that I had come back down by car and he had given me permission to do so.

He asked, 'Did you have anything to do with it?'

'No,' I said, 'I'm completely innocent.' But he wouldn't believe me and was giving me the third degree because the English committee were on his back.

I ended the conversation by saying, 'I didn't know anything about it. If you ring the English Union you can tell them I apologise, it was a dreadful mistake and I wouldn't have signed it if I'd known it was their crossbar.'

I went up to the village to buy a paper and it was on the front page of the *Times*. You know it's serious when it's on the front page of the *Times*. The story ran and ran. The English Rugby Union were furious that their crossbar had been cut down and they wanted retribution and they wanted the police to arrest the culprits and to jail them. So, on the Wednesday, I had a visit from our local policeman and a detective. They came to my sawmills and both of them had big grins on their faces. Reuters had got hold of the story and it was in all of the newspapers – it had even spread to South Africa and New Zealand. They say that when you're in a hole you should stop digging. I think the English Rugby Union should have stopped there because they were now becoming a laughing stock. It was a huge laugh for all the Welsh supporters.

The police constable said to me, 'It's a bloody good story.

You know we've come to see you officially to ask who were those people and would you recognise them again?'

I said, 'Well, they had Valley accents, maybe Pontypool or Pontypridd, I don't really know; they were from that way somewhere. I don't think I could recognise them because the three of them had red scarves on.'

The three of us had a good laugh about that and off they went. They were not really interested in who did it because it was such a hilarious moment.

It ran for another two days which meant it had been big news for the whole of the week. Thankfully, by the weekend, it had died down and the English realised that they had made a mistake. That was that until, on the following Tuesday afternoon, this old codger got up in the House of Lords and asked, 'What is the Home Secretary doing about the desecration of HQ when the Welsh barbarians crossed the border and cut the crossbar down? And what are the police doing about it?'

There it was, on the run again, filling the front pages once more.

Not one to miss an opportunity, I thought I could get some good publicity out of the situation. Following a brainwave I thought, 'I'm a timber merchant, what if I offered to replace the crossbar?'

So I went down to the village post office and I sent the English Rugby Union a telegram reading, 'Willing to replace crossbar, please inform if you accept,' and off it went.

Now when you send a telegram in a village like Bynea, as in all small villages I suppose, within 30 seconds everybody knows you've sent a telegram and the contents of it. So there we were, the whole village holding its breath for the reply from the English Rugby Union at Twickenham. Nothing came.

Time passed and, after two months or so, the whole story had died down when I found myself playing for the Barbarians against Leicester in Welford Road. After the game I sat down for a meal when who should be sitting two places down from me but one of the English selectors who was also on the Barbarians committee.

A mischievous grin came over my face and I leaned over and said, 'I sent the English Rugby Union a telegram about the crossbar but you didn't reply.'

He looked down his nose at me and replied, 'My dear chap, did you honestly think for a minute that we would ever have a Welsh crossbar at Twickenham?'

To be honest I was deflated and then he added, 'Furthermore, our president, Sir Wavell Wakefield, has deleted you from his list of invitees for Champers at Twickers with Wakers!'

That killed me and I couldn't stop laughing for a week!

As a postscript to all this, until fairly recently one section of the crossbar was displayed behind the bar of a pub at Cresswell Quay in Pembroke – it may still be there – but no-one seems to know what became of the other two sections.

There was another twist in that Twickenham game that I will share. On the Wednesday after the game the postman came to my parents' house with a parcel for me. My mother signed for it and the postman said, 'I don't know what's in it but it smells dreadful.'

So my mother took the parcel in and it did smell a bit vile. So she opened it up and inside there was a chicken along with a little note which said, 'Just something to congratulate you upon the great game at Twickenham. From a Neath supporter.'

Later that season this chap approached me after the Llanelli-Neath game and introduced himself as 'the one who sent you a chicken'.

'Good God,' I said. 'Why did you send me a chicken?'

'Well,' he said, 'We were coming out of Twickenham and we were thrilled. We hadn't won but we were still thrilled with a draw. I was passing this butcher's shop and I thought I would send you something. So we went in, picked out a chicken and he packed it for me and I posted it."

I suppose he'd had a few drinks and thought it was a good idea to send me this bloody chicken, not considering how long it would take to reach me.

We went on to beat Scotland and Ireland that season and, despite losing out in France, we finished runner-up to England in the championship. You could say that crossbar had robbed us of the opportunity of not only a Triple Crown but winning the championship as well. I'm glad they cut it down!

The following 1959 season was a mediocre affair for Wales. Despite getting off to the best possible start with revenge and a 5–0 victory over England in Cardiff, we lost the next game away to Scotland. I can tell you that it is no fun facing that long train journey home when the carriages are packed with disappointed Welsh rugby fans. We made amends by beating Ireland in Cardiff but were then well beaten away to France to bring the season to a disappointing close.

One thing that stood out when we played against Ireland was that the Welsh weather was so bad that we had to change our strip at half-time. It was the first time ever that Wales had had to undertake such a task. As I was coming out of the dressing room after the game, there were some 20 or so young students waiting for autographs. I spotted their teacher and asked where they were from, and he replied Canada. They had come all the way to Wales on a trip to see the game and experience the atmosphere in the Arms Park.

I asked, 'Have you had a good trip?'

They said it had been marvellous and they would remember it forever.

Then I got one of my Welsh jerseys out of my bag and asked if they wanted it as a souvenir. They were absolutely thrilled and the teacher in charge said it had made the trip for all of them, before promising to put it on display back in Vancouver University.

We beat the Irish that day by 6–3 after I had managed to kick two penalty goals from out of this mud heap, which earned me the Man of the Match award. It was a sign of the times that to mark the achievement I was awarded a cigarette lighter by some company who had sponsored it! I had it initialled and gave it to my girlfriend, who is now my wife, and she still has it.

CHAPTER 12

Len

LIFE HAS BEEN more than good to me but like almost everyone there have been hard times along the way – no more so than when I lost my brother Len. It is a phrase that is often heard but when someone loses their life, rugby is put in perspective and you realise it is only a game.

Len passed away on 23 September 1957, in Morriston hospital, aged 26. One of my saddest regrets in life was that I wasn't with him when he passed away. I had gone in the morning to collect my other brother, Roy, out of hospital – he was also in Morriston having a knee operation – and I popped in to see Len before picking Roy up. He was looking a little bit downcast and he asked if I could I stay with him. Of course, I had no idea how ill he was at that time and I said in my ignorance, 'I've got to pick Roy up and then I've got to go home; we've got a game tonight against Neath. I'll pop back later to see you after the game.'

He looked at me and said, 'OK.'

That was the last time I saw him alive because he died at 4 o'clock in the afternoon on that Tuesday. I keep chastising myself over why I didn't stay with him.

The news of his passing was supposed to have been broken to us by two policemen but when they arrived outside the house they couldn't face breaking the news, so they asked our next door neighbour if she would do it. There was a knock and when I came to the back door she was crying and telling me that the two policemen couldn't come in and that my brother had died and I had to go in and tell the family.

Later I had to drive up to Morriston hospital to formally identify him; it was a very sad time.

It is still a little difficult to talk about it because it was such a traumatic event in the family – my mother never got over it. There was a period just after Len's death when I had quite a job to concentrate on my career in rugby because I wanted to blame something or other, and so I blamed rugby. I used to think, did he become ill because he had a kick or something in a game? Of course, that wasn't the case because it was leukaemia; a disorder of the blood. On reflection, Len was probably the weakest of us as children growing up. At that particular time he always had colds and was away from school a lot. However, as he got to his late teens he was fit enough to blossom and do his National Service with no problems and he became a very talented rugby player. In fact, when I reflect on it, his talent went to the two games, rugby and football. He may have followed my father because he was a superb soccer player and I'm quite sure that if he'd stuck to soccer he would have gone far because he was quite a presence on the field.

I suppose Len and I were the closest of the family. If there were any quarrels he'd be the arbitrator, always with a level head and always with his two feet on the ground. I admired him greatly. When I was injured and told there was no future for me in the game, it was a very sad part of my life but then it brightened up when Len got his first cap. I was standing on the terrace at St Helen's singing the national anthem and I was crying my eyes out; it was a very emotional moment for me and one I shall never forget.

After Len won his cap, Bynea Rugby Football Club arranged a special presentation night for the both of us, which was a nice gesture, and I've still got a small cutting from the local newspaper.

And it wasn't just in sport that I was proud of my brother. I remember once, when Llanelli were playing London Welsh, Richard Burton – who was a huge rugby fan – and Elizabeth

Taylor came to see the game. Afterwards, they went into the clubhouse for a few drinks. Burton was chatting to Len and they swapped ties. That was the kind of man Len was, able to mix with Hollywood royalty as easily as his team-mates.

As Len became ill I had returned to play rugby and I think his life merged with mine at that particular time. He was ill in bed and back and forth to hospital. I felt helpless. Then I considered turning to rugby league in order to get some money to try and help Len. However Dr Gordon Rowley, the surgeon who had got me back into rugby again, got to hear of my plan and, following an international in Cardiff, he wanted to talk to me.

'Sit down there, I want to speak to you,' he said in the usual blunt manner that these people have. 'If you are looking to go North for money to save your brother don't bother, there is not a chance for him.'

This was the first indication that I got that Len was going to die and, naturally, I was taken aback. I was in turmoil but I couldn't tell the family because it would have crucified them. My mother, in particular, was always hopeful that the next day would be better.

Despite all the years I still get emotional when I think of Len and I miss him very much. But then I see him every day, as I have a large photograph of Len and I together, hanging on my dining room wall, and it's a strange thing but, when I look at it, his eyes seem to follow me.

When I became chairman of the Llanelli Former Players' Association and Stradey Park was demolished for new homes following the move to the new Parc y Scarlets stadium, I was really saddened that so much of our history had been lost. Then, as I was passing the picture, it was as if he was looking at me saying, 'What are you going to do about it? Are you just going to let Stradey go without any recognition?'

He was right of course and since then I have tried to do something about it. We are in the process of doing quite a bit to remember Stradey, and now his eyes are not so accusing when I pass them.

My other big regret in life is that we never managed to play for our country together, not even for Llanelli. We managed to play for the village together on a few occasions but never for Wales and that is a huge regret as far as I'm concerned. And there is also the fact that Len was on the shortlist for the 1955 Lions tour of South Africa. They had asked him if he would be available but he then missed the last Welsh game of the season, when he became ill, and so he was overlooked. I had also been sounded out as to my availability but, of course, my shoulder had ruled me out of the game. It would have been quite something to have had two British Lions in the family, that's for sure.

One of my fondest memories goes back to the one and only holiday we had as kids, when my grandmother paid for us to go to Aberystwyth. We caught a train to Carmarthen, where we changed for Aberystwyth, and I can still remember our great excitement as we leaned out the window and watched all the little stations go by along the way. I must have been about seven years of age and we really had an outstanding holiday. We didn't really do much but Len and I fed the seagulls on the pier every morning. We'd go down with a bag of breadcrumbs and we would hold them up and the seagulls used to swoop down and take it out of our hands.

My mother's great story was that one afternoon that week, as we were coming home late to our bed and breakfast place, Len and I were kicking a tin can along the street. I heard my mother chastise us because shoes were expensive in those days and we were scuffing them along the floor, when a gentleman passing by said, 'Leave them alone, let them kick the tin can, they could play for Wales one day.' Little did he know that both Len and I would see that dream come true.

There was a great deal of respect for Len in Llanelli and when he was buried around 2,000 people came to the village to pay their final respects, including his good friend Jim Griffiths, a Member of Parliament and the first ever Secretary of State for Wales, who had come down from London.

The only sour note was the fact that a charity game had been arranged by Llanelli Rugby Football Club to help Len out, with him not being able to work. It would have helped a lot. It had been arranged for the end of the season, which was not far away, but when Len passed it was cancelled. Of course, they could have continued with the game as the family could have done with a bit of money at that time to help with the funeral expenses and so on. It would also have been a chance for the supporters and players to show their respect to Len. Sadly, the decision to forget all about it was typical of how the clubs were run in those days.

CHAPTER 13

The Barbarian Lifestyle

ONE OF THE joys of playing rugby is being able to travel abroad and experience different lifestyles and cultures and, while my trips to Romania and Russia were eye-openers for the wrong reasons, I was fortunate enough to enjoy two overseas tours with the Barbarians.

If I am not mistaken I was part of the first two major tours – to Canada in 1957 and to South Africa in 1958 – that the famous invitation side undertook since being formed in 1890. We visited Canada in April and May and played six matches in Ontario, British Columbia and Quebec, winning them all quite comfortably but, back then, it was more of a missionary tour.

Once again we nearly came to grief on the flight over! We took off from Heathrow and flew up to Prestwick in Scotland, refuelled, and off we went to Canada. Now there was never enough fuel to reach anywhere of note in Canada and we just about had enough to set down in a place called Goose Bay, where they used to refuel the old Falcon planes which gave us security in those days. As we touched down we saw that ploughs had moved the snow to make 30-foot-high drifts either side of the runway. There were some huts at the far end, where we could have a cup of tea and whatever. I made the error of just putting my blazer on and climbing out of the plane; it must have been about 20 degrees Fahrenheit below because we were freezing. We had to run like hell to those huts. We got inside and thankfully there were two great big

119

red-hot potbellied stoves. We all gathered around with cups of steaming tea to warm our hands.

Canada is a beautiful country and, as part of the Commonwealth, was very welcoming and full of expatriates. We were well looked after by this millionaire who had made his money in the timber business and he took us by boat up into the Rockies to see the vast forests. He then showed us his timber mill. They had these huge saws, five in a row, cutting up these trunks over ten feet thick. Looking back, I should have spoken to him about my little timber business back in Bynea.

When it came to the matches, what stood out for me was that British Columbia selected a flanker with only one arm! That is no joke, but the remarkable thing about it was he was bloody marvellous. He was adept at handling the ball with one hand and he was a big threat throughout the game. It was amazing. I have never seen anything like it since.

When I arrived in Toronto I bumped into a chap by the name of Gwyn John – who had emigrated from Bynea with his wife several years before – who came to see me in the first game and invited me to go to his home and have a meal with his family. I went and we had a very pleasant evening. They had just had a little girl and I was cradling the baby on the settee when he took a picture on one of those instant cameras. He gave the photograph to me and when I arrived home it ended up in a drawer somewhere. Around 30 years later I was in Stradey Park on a Friday night and I went up to the bar to order a round of drinks, and there was this Canadian girl working behind the bar. I asked her which part of Canada she came from and she said Toronto. I asked what was she doing in Llanelli and she said, 'I've come to visit my father in Bynea.'

'What's his name?' I asked.

'It's Gwyn John.' She was the little baby I had cradled all those years ago!

I said, 'If you are here next Friday, I'll bring you a photograph which you will appreciate.'

I brought the photograph the following week and she was thrilled to think how coincidences come into your life.

In January 1958 Wales played Australia in Cardiff. The score was 6–3 and I kicked two penalty goals to win it. What stands out is that I was in a spot of bother with the WRU prior to the game because I had been asked by the legendary Irish wing Tony O'Reilly to play for the Irish Greyhounds over in Ireland. Now you are supposed to wrap yourself up in cotton wool a week before an international but I fancied a trip across the Irish Sea. I travelled over to Tipperary of all places for the evening game, I think it was on the Thursday, and they put me down as A N Other. I ended up playing a couple of days before an international and having to make a mad dash back home. I had a good ticking off as they say but, thankfully, was allowed to take my place in the side.

The remarkable thing about the Australia game was that I was joined by five of my Llanelli team-mates. The backline was virtually Llanelli, with myself at fullback, Ray Williams on the wing, Cyril Davies at centre, Carwyn James at outside-half and Wynne Evans at scrum-half. My old pal R H Williams was in the second row bringing the count up to six.

Carwyn was making his debut. He only won two caps for Wales but, then again, he was up against the magical Cliff Morgan. Cliff Morgan was a great outside-half. He was very quick but on top of that he was great company, he was brilliant. He was from the Valleys and his team talks before the game, when he was captain, were along the lines of: all the miners and steelworkers have been saving their money all year to come and watch us play and we were not going to let them down. He didn't go on about tactics, just the responsibility for winning the game for all these people.

Also making his Wales debut that day, inside Carwyn, was Wynne Evans. Those halfbacks had another, less dubious link – they were both chain-smokers. You may remember me describing Wynne training down Stradey with a cigarette in his mouth. Whenever we used to go anywhere they would be, sat next to each other, at the front of the bus and there would be this great big pall of smoke surrounding them and a coughing driver!

I shared a hotel room with Wynne Evans the night before the game. As it was his first cap he was awake most of the night chain-smoking in bed. He was also a big fan of Westerns, so he had the light on reading cowboy books all night. Neither of us had much sleep.

After that season's Five Nations it was back to the Barbarians. The tour to South Africa was a much more brutal affair than the Canada trip – even the outward-bound flight was not for the faint-hearted. We took a plane from Heathrow and landed to refuel in Khartoum. It was so hot when we left the plane that we had to run for the shelter of the buildings because our feet were boiling. The tarmacadam was sticking to our feet; it was not a very pleasant place altogether.

When we arrived in Johannesburg we stayed in a superb hotel which had quite a lot of history to it. There were wagon wheels from the first Boers' trek to South Africa, decorating its very large bar. We were told that all the big gold strikes in Johannesburg back in days gone by were all celebrated in this bar. Our hosts must have looked at my CV and had seen that I'd spent time working in the mines, as I was invited to visit the Robinson Deep Gold Mine. It was quite an event. We shot down two or three thousand feet and made our way to where the precious gold was being dug out of a small seam. As we made our way down this tunnel, which was very dimly lit, you could see the whites of the eyes and teeth of workers flashing in the headlamp on your hard hat as you passed them by. Later on we came across some workers in a railway truck, which was full of spoil. There must have been about 30 people with small shovels shovelling this rubble out. I asked,

'Wouldn't you be better off modernising this system and have what they have in the coal mines of Great Britain, where the truck is tipped over or you get trap doors that you just open so that you don't have to shovel out?'

And the chap replied, 'You know, we could modernise but we've got to give jobs out because if we don't allow the people to work, we'd have a lot of trouble.'

Of course, apartheid was at its height back then and before we left for South Africa we had a visit from a man from the Foreign Office who insisted we mustn't speak about the apartheid or have anything to do with the locals. You were not allowed to speak to coloured people; it was a no-go area. Years later teams refused to tour South Africa because the situation had become so bad but we didn't really consider not going. You need to remember it was in the days before cheap foreign travel and the chance to tour such a country was a chance of a lifetime, especially for a working-class boy from Bynea.

After we arrived in Johannesburg we were invited to a civic reception in the Mayoral Parlour where we were reminded by a British Embassy gentleman not to speak about politics or get caught up in anything unsavoury as we could lay ourselves open to headlines in the papers the next day.

Our first game was against the Transvaal in Eden Park. There must have been 80,000 to 90,000 in the crowd. It was a bright warm sunny day and the pitch was as hard as a rock. I remember their outside-half put in an up-and-under but I couldn't get to it in time and it landed and then flew up about 30 feet in the air and bounced back towards the opposition – that was my first experience of hard grounds in South Africa.

Also, because of the altitude, I found that you could kick great distances through the thin air. Once I marked the ball under my own posts and decided to give it a good old whack and, lo and behold, it went into touch on their 25, which must have been all of 75 yards. There wasn't a murmur from the crowd because they'd seen it all before.

The unusual thing about that game was that there were no coloured people allowed in to see it. However, at one end of the ground, where there was just a bank instead of a stand, some trees had grown higher than the top of the bank and in them were 20 to 30 coloured children, all hanging from these branches to catch sight of the game.

We were based for most of the trip in Cape Town, which is probably the nicest place we visited in South Africa, and dominated by Table Mountain. One of the boys, Gareth Griffiths, and myself decided to make it to the top. The last leg was taken by a very rickety cable-car-type thing, which was more like a garden shed with a couple of windows, in which you sat on these wooden benches hanging on for dear life. But having got to the top there was a brilliant view all the way around. You could see where the Indian Ocean met the Atlantic and that was an amazing sight.

Once I set off to do a bit of exploring on my own. I decided to catch a bus and climbed aboard and found a seat. Suddenly, the conductor came up to me – I was sitting in the back of the bus which was full of coloured people, and he appeared very embarrassed.

He said, 'Sir, you will have to get off.'

'Why is that?' I asked.

'This is a coloured bus. We are not allowed on white buses and you're not allowed on our bus.' So there we are; I had to get off and catch a white bus.

At this time there was a curfew in place which meant all coloured people had to be indoors by 9 o'clock. I found that very difficult to come to terms with. I had met some really genuine, well-educated people, who all had to be restricted in this manner just because of the colour of their skin – it was a very difficult time.

Of course, we didn't always listen to the advice. One of our forwards, who shall remain nameless, was very taken with a pretty chambermaid who worked in our hotel. He somehow managed to borrow a car and took her for a drive, breaking the curfew. They parked up in a lay-by somewhere and things were getting steamed up in the car when there was a sharp knock on the window. He wiped the window to see a giant policeman pointing a torch in his face.

'What's going on here?' the policeman asked.

'Just a bit of necking,' replied our player.

The policeman must have recognised his Barbarians blazer or something because he gave him the benefit of the doubt and said, 'Well tuck you neck back into your pants and get back to your hotel!'

Not surprisingly, that player became known to us all as Neckie after that!

One of the most enjoyable aspects of my tour to South Africa was meeting up with an old friend of mine, Ken James, who hailed from Hendy, a village near Llanelli. Now Ken had done his National Service at the same time as me and, having played a few games for Aberavon, he was part and parcel of the Devonport Services team. He eventually emigrated to Rhodesia with his wife. When he heard that I was on the Barbarians tour, he drove some 300 miles or so in the hope of meeting up.

He turned up at our hotel after our final match and on our last night before flying home. Over the moon to see him I said, 'It's a pity we've only got a few minutes because I've got to go to the post-match dinner.' Then I had an idea and said, 'I'll tell you what, I've got a spare blazer. If you put it on nobody will notice and you can sit next to me at the dinner.'

The plan worked a treat and we had a marvellous time, all the drinks were free and flowing – it really was a terrific reunion. The odd thing was that nobody actually enquired who my friend was until the following day when Tony O'Reilly asked, 'Who was that guy sitting next to you last night?' When I told him who it was he had a huge laugh about it.

The other thing I remember about the trip to South Africa

was bringing my father back a large carton of duty-free cigarettes. Like a lot of people back then he used to smoke and he gratefully took them up to his favourite haunt, the British Legion club. He would pass a few around but the rest he smoked in about three months. When he developed a bad cough, I took him to the doctor who told him that he had to give up smoking, no more cigarettes. It was going to be a huge problem for my father who said. 'Duw, Duw. I've still got 500 of those king size left.'

The doctor said, 'I don't care, you can't smoke them.'

My father thought and asked, 'What about a pipe then?'

The doctor said, 'Well yes, if you're desperate, you smoke a pipe.'

When I visited my father the next day he was sitting on the settee smoking his pipe but actually what he had done was jammed the cigarettes into the pipe shaft so he could smoke them. I thought to myself, 'You can't win here.'

Our record on tour was three wins, one draw and two losses: Transvaal (17–17), Western Transvaal (11–3), Western Province (9–8), Northern Transvaal (9–13), Combined Transvaal (16–18) and East Africa (52–12).

Not a bad record considering we were playing for the Barbarians and the traditional style is to run everything and we were determined not to change that philosophy. That, of course, led to mistakes and the massive South Africans would pounce on them to kill us off. When you went to the bar after the game you would be dwarfed by the South African players. If you wanted to win you would have to keep it tighter and confront the forwards, but, as I said, in the true Barbarian spirit it was something we refused to do.

CHAPTER 14

Becoming a British and Irish Lion

As PLAYERS WE had more reason than usual to rue a mixed Five Nations championship in 1959 as it was a Lions year and, following that final whistle, many of us faced a nervous wait to see if we had made it onto the plane bound for Australia and New Zealand.

So when the letter arrived in Bynea, with the invitation to be part of the tour, I was thrilled. It was brilliant to play for Wales, absolutely, and it was great to play for the Barbarians but the ultimate selection was to be asked to be a member of the British and Irish Lions touring team. It is the pinnacle of every rugby player's dream; if you're selected then you are the best in Great Britain and Ireland.

I was so thrilled because, after many trials, tribulations and bad injuries, I had finally achieved my ambition.

Financially, it was a far cry from the professional world of today's Lions, who stand to earn upwards of £60,000 each if they win the Test series and have every conceivable need taken care of by the coaching and support staff. In 1959 we had no coaches, no back-up staff, and we looked after our own kit. I had given up my timber business to go on the tour and we were paid a paltry 50p a day, which was not much even back then, and don't forget we were away for five months. But we managed to get by and enjoy ourselves thoroughly – I wouldn't have changed it for the world.

We met at the beginning of May in Eastbourne to have a

week's training before getting on the plane. They were quite hard sessions. We were doing two a day and the grounds were very hard at that time of the year. We had taken about a month off from the end of the season, after being told to take a rest, which I think was an error because your fitness dropped off and all these training sessions caused you problems. There were lots of tight muscles. There was no real organisation and no physio to help. We simply met in the hotel and trained twice a day. And that was it.

It was a good bonding exercise, I suppose, but I had already played with a large number of the team on the two tours with the Barbarians, so I was familiar with many of the faces.

We left Heathrow in the last week of May, bound for Australia, and were the first British Lions to fly anywhere. Previously everyone had gone by boat. Once again the flight was pretty hairy. The four-propeller plane could only fly for five hours or so before having to land to refuel. To make matters worse, we had major problems with the plane. Each time we landed there seemed to be a six-hour delay for repairs.

First of all we landed in Zurich, then in Beirut before touching down in Karachi, Calcutta and Bangkok. We had a 24-hour stop in Darwin because one of the engines had fallen off, or something like that, and we needed a new engine before we could go down to Melbourne. It was a huge trek. We set off at 12 o'clock on a Saturday and we didn't arrive in Melbourne until 10.30am on the Tuesday morning.

When we landed in Karachi in Pakistan in the dark we bounced all over the place. We must have bounced about 20 times. The cases fell down from the overhead lockers in the cabin and the drinks trolley flew down the alleyway. When we got out of the plane we could see reels of barbed wire wrapped around the wheels. The pilot had tried to land before the runway started and had taken up the fencing which surrounded the airfield. We were delayed for about six hours before we eventually left again. This was the case throughout the trip.

We flew into Darwin on three engines and we came in low over what I can only describe as a shanty town. All the houses had tin sheet roofing which was all rusting. It was quite a sight. We were greeted by scorching weather and an indifferent sporting public. Rugby was not the most popular game in Australia in those days – as is still the case – and we therefore had small crowds.

When we arrived in Melbourne we didn't know what day it was as it had been a pretty horrendous journey altogether and, here we were, set to play our first game in four days' time. With the change of time zones you couldn't get to sleep – as you would be tired in the day and you were wide awake at night – so it took a little bit of time to get used to the changeover. We then stayed in Coogee Bay, which is adjacent to Bondi Beach, and with great excitement we went for a swim because that was the thing to do. There were great big waves chopping you down; what an experience that was!

Our first game, against Victoria in Melbourne, was an evening kick-off and it was very easy. We ran out winners by 53 points to 18. I didn't play and watched from the stand. Sat about three seats away from me was a Llanelli lad by the name of Gerry Watkins. He introduced himself and we had a good chat; he had emigrated out there but later got a bit nostalgic and returned home.

In the 1950s Australians, especially the older generation, were very suspicious of the Poms, as they used to call us. There was very little holiday travel in those days and not a lot of British people came to visit and so we were viewed with derision at times. If one of our team got injured, and he was lying on the floor, the home crowd would be delighted. It was the first time I'd come across a crowd cheering when a person was injured.

I made my Lions debut in the game against New South

Wales in Sydney. It wasn't a very good day for us as we came up against a very strong side that was virtually the entire Australian team. In the first three minutes of the game Niall Brophy, our wing, broke his ankle and was carried off. In those days there were no substitutes so we were really up against it. Then I pulled a hamstring and had to hobble around for the last 20 minutes which didn't do much good at all. It was a very tight game, in very warm temperatures, and in the end we lost by 18 points to 14. We were caught out really and it was not the result I would have liked to mark such a major milestone in my career.

We then travelled up to Queensland. We were accommodated in Brisbane and it was very pleasant with the temperature around 80 degrees Fahrenheit all the year round. Today the area is famous for its Gold Coast, a huge strip of land running out into the sea with gorgeous beaches, but when we were there it only had one hotel, the Hilton, now it is saturated with them. On the first evening we were invited to see a show starring a British girl called Sabrina. She'd starred in films with the comedian Arthur Askey and she was the original sweater girl – her attributes were huge and she was a very nice looking girl!

I missed a pretty easy victory against Queensland, by 39 points to 11, and was once again confined to the stands for the first Test in Brisbane as I had still not recovered from my injury. As a team, however, we were beginning to find our rhythm and we now had a supreme three-quarter line that was very quick, with four members of the team able do 100 yards in ten seconds or less, and on these dry grounds they couldn't touch us. We ran out winners by 17 points to 6.

I had recovered sufficiently to be selected for our next game against New South Wales Country in a place called Tamworth. We had flown in by Dakota and it had taken us ages to get there. It was a wide open town in the middle of sheep country. The streets were more than 50 yards wide, with wooden walkways along each side. As I walked down the street I saw a barber's and decided to have a haircut as it was getting a bit long. I sat in the chair and asked for a trim. When I saw myself in the mirror afterwards I was practically bald!

I asked the barber, 'Good God, what's your job?'

He replied, 'This is my spare time job, I'm a sheep shearer during the shearing period.'

Later that day we ran out winners by 27 points to 14 in blazing sunshine which left my exposed scalp sunburnt! I remember it being an awkward game as it was the first time I'd come across what they call the blocking system, where their players blocked you from tackling another player. It was illegal but the referee didn't seem to mind, which was very frustrating and caused a lot of problems. Eventually, the use of the elbow did the trick.

Then I was flattened by one of their forwards with the words ringing in my ear, 'Got you, you Pommie bastard.' It didn't go down very well when I said, 'At least I know who my father is and where he came from!'

We arrived in Sydney for the second Test with half of our players down with various injuries, mainly pulled muscles, which we put down to the hard grounds and us not being used to them. They were like concrete and all the players were having these burns when we fell and skidded along. In the end we had to revert to wearing women's underwear to keep our hips from being cut up when they scraped along the floor!

My hamstring was playing up again and I was one of 15 players who had to get medical attention before the game and was not passed fit to play, which was extremely frustrating.

With our squad decimated, Bryn Meredith – who was probably the best hooker in the world at that time but couldn't get a place in the front row because our captain, the Irishman Ronnie Dawson, had to play there – was tried out at wing forward. He had only been on the field for about 20 minutes when he pulled a muscle and had to leave. Next we lost our scrum-half, Stan Coughtrie, before John Young, our speedy wing, went down with another pulled muscle! We were so pleased when the rain came down and cooled everything off, which was much to our advantage. We were down to 12 men but we managed to hold on and come out with a 24–3 win.

I must admit that Ken Scotland, who was my rival for the fullback jersey, was superb. He was only 11 stone 8, but he was so quick and agile, I admired his game greatly.

On the Sunday morning we got ourselves together and went to Sydney Airport to catch our flight to New Zealand for the business end of the tour. Not surprisingly, there weren't many people there to wave us goodbye. However, as we were waiting quietly for our flight, out of the blue, coming in from New Zealand, we spotted Sir Edmund Hillary and his wife. To our delight they came over to talk to us. He was a brilliant man altogether and I was so pleased to shake his hand and say what a marvellous thing he had done six years previously in climbing Everest. Before we left he warned us about the dirty tricks of the All Blacks' forwards and predicted that we would have a torrid time in New Zealand. Unsurprisingly his words came true!

The flight across the Tasman Sea had been very up and down, and, true to form, we were hit by an electric storm. A lot of people on the plane were feeling very sick, so it was a relief to get to Auckland.

Arriving in New Zealand was the complete opposite of arriving in Australia. The airport was crammed with people; they were hanging from the rafters. There must have been 25,000 there. It really was a huge welcome. A Maori girl sang 'Haere Mai', which is the traditional welcome to New Zealand, and it was lovely. We were then taken outside and put into open-top vintage cars and driven into Auckland where there were masses of people on the pavements waving and cheering. What a difference compared to Australia. It was a magnificent welcome, like being a film star in Hollywood.

The next day we had a reception with various dignitaries, including the Prime Minister of New Zealand, Walter Nash. It was funny because he called me over because I was Welsh. We talked and he asked me what part of Wales I was from. When I said Llanelli he told me his grandfather was Welsh and he still had relatives near Maesteg. He then asked how far Llanelli was from Maesteg. When I said about 20 miles he replied, 'You might know them, the Joneses.' I didn't have the heart to tell him there were around 300,000 Joneses in Wales!

Our first game in New Zealand was against Hawke's Bay in Napier. We won comfortably, by 52 points to 12, but it was matters off the field that remain in my memory. It was one of the poorer grounds in the country and only had one main stand; the rest of the people would stand around the touchline. However, to accommodate such a huge crowd as we had attracted, they erected what I'd call scaffolding stands for the full length of the touchline, about 120 yards. You would get scaffolding put up and then planks were laid on it and people sat on that.

There were 2,000 people packed into these stands and they rose up to about 20 tiers. When we attacked down the side of the field, the excitement would make the supporters rise onto their feet and they would be coming with you, like a wave. The whole stand would sway towards the end of the field. It was the first time I saw stretcher-bearers in place for the crowds because they were there to carry people who had fallen off the ends of the stands. I had never seen that before. As the game got more exciting, more and more people were dropping off the end. It was like a battlefield.

By now, as a squad, we were really starting to gel together socially as well as on the rugby field and we were developing into very good ambassadors for the Lions. Fortunately, we didn't have one awkward person amongst us; we all seemed to be compatible, which was quite unusual for a group of people who are together for such a long period of time. We had our big characters of course who kept you going, none more so than Ray Prosser who would tell us great stories about his Pontypool escapades and was one half of the most unlikely pairings, along with Harlequins and English second row David Marques. Now Prosser would use three swear words to every one word of the Queen's English, while Marques was Cambridge educated and could trace his family back to Magna Carta, yet they were always room-mates. Prosser would wear Marques' top hat and tails and try to impersonate him! Years later I asked David Marques how they had gotten on so well and he said, 'I was fascinated by the chap. He taught me a whole new language I didn't know existed!'

I remember little things like having breakfast together – you would get up early as training would be in the morning, and then at 3 o'clock in the afternoon. On one occasion Tony O'Reilly and Andy Mulligan were discussing Greek mythology and Ray Prosser was sitting at their table listening intently. He didn't stop eating, he always had two of everything, a huge breakfast, and suddenly at the end of the conversation he turned and said to Bryn Meredith, 'Duw Bryn, isn't education great for you. It teaches you to say words like marmalade and corrugated.' That brought the house down. For all your education a little bit of Ray Prosser brought you down to earth.

Tony O'Reilly and Andy Mulligan were also great comedians together and constantly took the mick out of the New Zealanders or our own management, who were not very good, it has to be said.

Our tour manager, Alf Wilson, was a very dour Scotsman who had this outdated theory about rugby players and how they should behave. He was old army and he couldn't quite come to terms with the fact that we were not army people. Neither were we children; we were young people enjoying ourselves in a new and exciting country. Talking of which, we came across a different system of drinking hours from back home. We had first seen it in Australia, where they used to call it the 6 o'clock swill – all the pubs closed at 6 o'clock. Everyone finished their work at 4 or 5 o'clock and rushed to the pubs and drank as much as they could before closing time. We thought that very strange because there was nothing to do after 6 o'clock. We came across a similar thing in New Zealand, where all the hotels closed at 9 o'clock so you couldn't get anything to eat. When we came back from the cinema or back from wherever we had been, the bar and restaurant would be shut. The staff were apologetic and offered to make us some toast or whatever was available at that time, but it seemed a crazy situation.

I must admit New Zealand at that time was a very macho, male dominated place. We would go to a rugby club and there would be this white chalk mark on the floor in front of the bar. I asked one of the hosts what it was for and he said that they had laws in the club that said no women were allowed beyond the white mark.

On the subject of pubs, when we had arrived in Timaru, not long into the tour, it was pouring with rain so we were unable to train. Neither my best friend and Llanelli team-mate Rhys Williams nor I had been picked for the midweek match against a combined South Canterbury, North Otago and Mid Canterbury side, so R H, as he was known to all, said to me, 'I fancy a pint.'

I agreed but we faced a bit of a dilemma as, besides the nasty habit of closing early in the evening, pubs were few and far between. However, we made enquiries and were told that there was a pub in a logging centre which was ten miles or so outside of town.

We borrowed an old car and off we went looking for this pub. When we got there we took a look at it, it was a typical dive, with everything sort of knackered. It had salon doors, sawdust on the floor and when we went in there was this huge, fat barman with a big bearded face behind the bar. We went up and I ordered two schooners of beer. The drinks were put on the bar and then the barman turned to me and said, 'He's drinking too.'

I looked around and there was nobody else there. Then he pointed at the floor. When I looked down, standing there next to me was a very large, white billy goat with pleading eyes. So I bought him a pint and put it on the sawdust floor and went to pay again and the barman said, 'He smokes as well.'

So I had to buy him a packet of cigarettes. Two hours' later the billy goat had drunk six pints of beer and munched 60 cigarettes. He had one hell of a cough and didn't have a leg under him. At one point we tried to teach him to sing 'Calon Lân', but by then he was too far gone! It's a great memory of a hilarious afternoon in the company of a chain-smoking, alcoholic billy goat.

One of the best things about touring is experiencing the way of life in countries different to your own. When we were in Poverty Bay we were invited to an outdoor shoot and I tasted swan for the first time – it was quite nice actually. I think it's against the law in our country to eat swan, unless you're the king or queen, but in New Zealand, when we visited, they were considered a pest because there were so many of them. When they colonised New Zealand they brought animals with them which escaped and ran free, and hence they had thousands of swans becoming pests, so they shot them.

Then we attempted what they called pig-sticking, which is hunting small wild boars with a kind of spear. However, although they were in profusion, we struggled through this bushy section of Gisborne and never came across any, which was fortunate because I didn't fancy sticking a pig. Wild deer were also a problem, as they used to come down from the hills and eat all the crops. Every little cottage would have this huge lamp at the back of it to draw the deer down. They would switch the lamp on and just shoot at the deer. That was Sunday lunch taken care of.

I played my first game in New Zealand in Gisborne, coming out on top 23–14 against a combined Poverty Bay/East Coast side. We then flew to Auckland for our next game. We knew it was going to be a tough one as Auckland contained virtually half of the New Zealand team. There was a huge crowd on that bright and sunny day. It looked as if most of the people had been queuing up all night because they had sleeping bags and whatever, a fact that was becoming quite common for our games. People would camp out at night just to be able to get into the ground the next day.

The game was a real stormer and we had to put up with a lot of aggravation from the Auckland forwards, especially from one gentleman by the name of Albert Prior who was really something nasty. He was their second row, a big Maori who was about 17 stone and about 6 foot 5 inches with several teeth missing, from the grin on his face, as he went about the business of mayhem with gusto, much to the annoyance of our forwards. As usual, the referee was always on the blind side and didn't penalise him or say anything to him throughout the game. It then became fractious but we managed to come out of the game with a very good win, 15–10, and I must say that it was one of the better games that we had played in New Zealand so far.

Halfway through the game David Marks, our second row, was trapped at the bottom of a ruck with his head sticking out near the ball; he couldn't move. Albert Prior ran around and danced on his head and face and then ran back to the other side again. The referee ignored it entirely, even when our trainer came on to patch up Marks, who had blood all over him. Marks was a proper English gentleman and, after the trainer had patched him up, he walked over and shook the hand of Albert Prior much to the amazement of us players and the 60,000 people in the crowd. After the game Ray Prosser asked, 'What did you want to shake his hand for?'

And Marks said, 'I wanted to show everybody what a cad he was.'

We then beat a New Zealand Universities side, 25–13, in Christchurch, before heading on to play Otago in Dunedin. The home team had a reputation for beating touring sides and it was a very tough game indeed and the very first one we lost in New Zealand. We were still carrying a large number of injuries, myself included, so it was a bad day at the office. It was just one of those days where everything went wrong for us. We were put under extreme pressure and panicked a bit and eventually lost quite heavily by 26 points to 6.

By the time we arrived in Timaru to play a combined South Canterbury, North Otago and Mid Canterbury side, I was getting myself fitter and I was selected for the game. We managed to get back on track as we ran out winners by 21 points to 11. We didn't play very well but it was one of those times when, even if you played badly, you stuck in there and got a result. It was my first outing for about two and a half weeks and I couldn't get myself into the game properly.

The next day we boarded a steam train which traversed the whole of South Island and took us to Southland. It took around nine hours to get from one end to the other, sitting in this rickety train made up of three or four wooden carriages. What amazed me about that journey was that whenever we passed a railway station there would be about a thousand children there waving to us. They must have come from outlying farms because there didn't seem to be a lot of housing around. We would pass by and they would all be waving and we had to poke our heads out of the window and say hello. It was the same when we made a stop; you would be swamped by a mass of people where you wouldn't expect a large population, they seemed to be coming from everywhere. The lovely thing was that when we stopped at a particular station it was like a huge party. There would be tables groaning under the weight of food the local people had prepared. We would have fried oysters and lamb chops dipped in batter – you could have been 20 stone coming out of there if you had not watched what you ate, because it really was a magnificent feast. It seemed to me the women in New Zealand wanted to outdo each other. I suppose after we left the crowd would suddenly dig in, it was marvellous.

Southland was at the bottom end of New Zealand, the closest point to Antarctica we had been and, not surprisingly, the weather wasn't very good there, it was a very cold place. I remember the game, played in Invercargill, being very cold and very muddy; it was a dreadful day. Ironically, despite wishing I was in the stand at times, we managed to survive to the end and come out 11–6 winners.

Being so far south did have one advantage and, late that night, I was one of the intrepids who travelled around 17 miles from where we were staying – arriving at 4 o'clock in the morning – to see the Aurora Australis or southern lights and the sun rising over the Antarctic. It is a sight that stays with you. New Zealand really is a spectacular country. The following day we took a bus ride all the way up to Queenstown to view a mountain range known as the Remarkables. Never was a mountain range so aptly named; they are truly a remarkable and beautiful sight altogether. It is days like this that make you realise how special playing rugby can be; I would never have seen sights like this had I not picked up a rugby ball.

The New Zealand public really took us to heart and we were welcomed everywhere we went. On one occasion we watched a great parade, a carnival-type occasion, pass our hotel with a long row of lorries. On one lorry there were some lions in a cage and a trainer, dressed as an All Black, was whipping them into submission. Another lorry came along with a pile of snow on it; it became a battle of people throwing snowballs at us. I think we replied with a fire hose from our hotel. Everyone was in hilariously good moods and it showed the rapport between us and the New Zealand people.

Before games we would be bombarded on radio programmes with what the home team was going to do to us – they were going to maul us, and we didn't have a hope, and all that nonsense. The newspapers would be full of how good they were and how bad we were. It was quite laughable really.

The first Test was at Carisbrook Stadium in Dunedin, and proved to be a huge draw for people. They had been queuing outside the ground from about noon the previous day; there were tents and huge amounts of people staying out all night just to get in first. There is a story about a builder who lived next door to the stadium, who lost all his ladders. There was a photograph in one of the newspapers the next day showing six ladders up against the wall. Those without tickets had stolen them to be able to look over the perimeter wall. There is also a picture of four supporters standing precariously on top of a tower of wooden pallets in order to get a view of the game. How they didn't injure themselves is miraculous – it looked like the leaning tower of Pisa!

We still hold the record for the number of people that watched us during that tour – 850,000 people came to our games, which was a third of the population of New Zealand at the time. The crowds were enormous – you could not get tickets. We'd play in a town with a population of 15,000 and there would be 30,000 watching the game.

From a personal point of view it was very frustrating because I was not available for selection yet again because of injury. As I have explained, life with the Lions was very different back then and there was no medical back up other than a cold sponge!

On the field we were to suffer a narrow defeat but to this day I'm convinced we were robbed by a biased home referee. We lost by 18 points to 17. We scored six tries that day, but the referee only gave four of them while he gave New Zealand numerous kicks at goal – including allowing one that didn't go over. One touch judge put his flag up but the other kept his down, the referee gave the kick to win the game! Remember back then a try was only worth three points. With today's scoring system we would have won 28–18! We outscored them four tries to nil.

The crowd erupted in boos and shouts of, 'Reds! Reds!' Not black. I have never seen that before, the crowd turning on the All Blacks. We had been robbed and the crowd knew it. When you are playing home referees there is not much you can do. One told me, 'I have to live here after you go home!'

Two weeks later we played against a combined West Coast and Buller side in a place called Greymouth. It was a midweek game on a sunny winter's day. We took to the field first and we had the normal cheer. Then their team came out and they had a cheer, and then this little fat referee ran out. He had the biggest cheer of the lot because he was obviously a favourite and I knew then that we had another problem. The game started. It had been going for 20 minutes when we scored a push-over try, but it was disallowed.

Then they had a drop-out on their 25. The ball went long to Tony O'Rilley, our very quick Irish wing who was to go on to become the record Lions' try scorer. Tony caught the ball. He was big lad, about 6 feet 3 inches and he went off like a rocket. I have not seen anything like it because he started sidestepping, which took him all the way across the field to the other touchline and then, suddenly, he was boxed in on that touchline so he started coming back again. Back he came to the other side. As Ray Prosser later said, 'He sidestepped me once and then he gave me a dummy.' But Tony was not finished; he battered his way through the middle of the field and over he went under the posts. After Tony put the ball down he said to the referee, 'I nearly scored that time.'

This poor fat referee had chased him everywhere and had no alternative but to give the try.

Despite not being 100 per cent fit I played in the 15–3 win

against Taranaki. I was feeling very frustrated by that time because I couldn't get myself going. I was being curtailed by injuries which were not serious enough to end my tour, but niggling injuries which made it difficult to get my form back. However, when the second Test in Wellington arrived, we had so many injuries I was really forced into having to play. Despite all that, it was a game that perhaps we should have won but, again, their giant fullback, Don Clark, who was known as The Boot and had kicked all the points in the first Test, was to deny us.

They probably knew that I wasn't really fit and five minutes into the game their outside-half put in this enormous up-and-under into the sun. I turned my back slightly, to take the sun out of my eyes, and I took it just over my shoulder and managed to get it back 40 yards down the field and into touch. That was my last up-and-under of the game.

Of that catch a New Zealand newspaper later wrote:

> We may have seen its equal but we have never seen a better take in such difficult circumstances. Running back to the ball, which had been kicked high and long, and then a half twist in the glaring sun, and perfect handling, it was in its way the gem of the game.

I suppose those skills I had perfected with the white-hot guttering and drainpipes in the Vitraflex factory had stood me in good stead!

It was a very tough game indeed and, towards the middle of the second half, I was really struggling with my leg injury. To top it all somebody hit me with a fierce tackle and I managed to get a dead leg, so I was really limping on both legs.

The rugby writer J B G Thomas wrote afterwards:

> It was a great day for Terry Davies. A big occasion man, he came back into the side to play a fierce Test after an absence of seven matches through injury without any preliminary workout, and early in the match, before the All Blacks had scored, he badly bruised a thigh muscle in a tackle.

We were still leading going into the last eight minutes of

the game but lost under quite controversial circumstances as far as I'm concerned. We were given a penalty near the halfway line and Ronnie Dawson, our captain, told me to kick it into touch. I said, 'Why don't I go for goal and we can run the clock down?' Even if I had missed we could have pressed up on them and kept them in their own half.

But he said, 'No, put it into touch.'

Of course I tried to kick it as long as I possibly could but ended up missing touch and then they came back at us. From a scrum on the halfway line our nemesis, Clarke, came in from fullback, made the extra man, and scored in the corner. Strictly speaking I should have got it into touch but there was a strong possibility I could have kicked the goal as well, which would have put us out of sight. As it was we lost by 11 points to 8.

As a footnote on our fitness worries, we firmly suspected that New Zealand had a spy in our camp, as it were. The tour had been very well organised by our hosts to give them the best possible advantage. They gave us two easy games and then they hit us with a really hard one and often they made us travel around 300 miles between each game, so they tired us out. It was really good tactics by them, I suppose. It wasn't like this when they were in Great Britain. You play fair. New Zealand, on the other hand, took every opportunity they could out of the system.

One of their ploys was to provide us with a baggage man for the tour, who acted as a spy. In fairness he was a nice little chap called Taffy Davies who had emigrated to New Zealand some 50 years earlier. He must have been in his early 70s but he was a superbly fit man who would leave the hotel at 7 o'clock in the morning, wherever we stayed, and run for an hour for his exercise. He was a great character. He was nominated by the New Zealand Rugby Union probably because of all the information he would slide back to them at some point or other – they knew all about our injuries and what we were doing. I suppose that was part and parcel of New Zealand rugby. The more information they had the better prepared they would be, they really had all the gen on us, you know.

Following the second Test Andy Mulligan and I were allowed to remain in Wellington for a week to have treatment, which was excellent I must admit, and we both had a great week there. We were entertained royally by the Wellington management. We stayed in a nice hotel and were invited out to sail with one of their Olympic yachtsmen. We had a great day sailing around just outside Wellington harbour. It was a windy day and we were challenged to sit in a little seat, at the end of some ropes coming down from the mast, that if the boat keeled over, it would swing you away from the boat. I took the challenge and, my God, what a challenge it was. There I was, swinging about 30 feet away from the side of the boat, with these huge waves crashing around me but, having been in the Marines, I was up to it.

By the time we arrived in Christchurch for the third Test my hamstring injury had flared up once more and I was ruled out of the game. I was gutted and, as a drastic measure, it was decided to give me a cortisone injection. It was a fairly new procedure in those days and I remember going to yet another hospital to have it. This doctor came along with a huge needle which he plunged into my thigh, going in about six inches. It took about ten days to work but suddenly it felt better and I must admit it cleared up any strains and niggles I had picked up on the tour. I thought to myself, why hadn't I had the injection six weeks ago? Unfortunately our management wasn't very good at looking after players and their injuries.

I must admit I never really had a proper conversation with our management throughout the whole tour – they seemed to be quite independent of the players. It was more or less the same for everyone. The whole side was going along with no contact of any kind from the management except for when we were on the bus, and then they would occupy the front seats. When I think about it we didn't have a coach, we just seemed to gel together in this free-flowing rugby, which was something that had captured the hearts of the New Zealand public. They were queuing up to see it, they were gorging themselves on a different style of rugby that had taken New Zealand by storm.

I think people back home were aware of what we were doing, but there was no widespread television and, while the games were on the radio back home, people would have to get up in the middle of the night to listen. The main reporting was left to a few journalists from home who had made the long trip over. Similarly, communicating with family at home was also difficult. There were no long-distance phone calls then. I used to write home once a week, but letters took a long time to get there and you'd receive one back every fortnight.

We didn't have supporters, you didn't really see many ex-pats in those days and, as I have explained, international travel was out of reach for your average supporter. At every game we played, the crowd was all one-sided, so we had to be mentally tough. The only Welshman I met in New Zealand was a young man who came to see me just before one game in Palmerston North. I was walking into the ground when he said to me, 'You're Terry Davies, aren't you?'

He was a chap called Alan Evans who was from Llwynhendy, the next village to Bynea. He said he had been in the Navy and had jumped ship to marry a girl from New Zealand. He came to see me to ask me to take a letter home to his parents – he hadn't had any contact with them because he was on the run! That's how his parents found out that he was alive and well and married in New Zealand – when I called on them when I returned home from the tour.

The third Test, played in Christchurch, was a real disaster and was perhaps our worst performance of the tour. The ground hadn't been a happy hunting ground for us as we'd lost there against Canterbury, 20–14, about three weeks earlier, and the third Test went the same way after New Zealand completely outplayed us, winning by 22 points to 8.

It was very disappointing for us because we should have won the first Test and at least drawn the second really. Now the whole series was lost and it looked as if we were going to be whitewashed. We were all very downhearted but on the Sunday things picked up again when O'Reilly and Mulligan did their little bit to cheer everybody up. We had a good laugh and decided to get on with it.

On a personal note my hamstring problems were finally beginning to clear up, helped in no small part to that cortisone injection and a bit of advice from the good Doctor Rowley who had been reading about my injury and sent a telegram telling me to place a piece of felt about half an inch thick in the boot of my damaged leg. The measure appeared to work a treat and once more my career was back on track, thanks to the Swansea doctor.

Our next game was against the Junior All Blacks and most of their players probably went on to be capped the following year for New Zealand. We won 29–9, but it was quite a good game and they tried very hard. I remember one instance when their wing, a local sprint champion, came flying into the corner and O'Reilly was on one side of him and I on the other. We eventually took him out with a big thump. Unfortunately, he fell between us and broke his leg. It was the first time in New Zealand that we'd managed to get one of their players off the field and gain a bit of an advantage.

Then came the New Zealand Maoris in Auckland. There we had a little bit of pay back on their second row forward, Albert Prior. You may recall he quite literally had a bit of 'prior', having been the instigator of a great deal of dirty stuff in an Auckland jersey at the beginning of the tour. It was the most bad-tempered game of the whole tour. It didn't do the Maori reputation much good because up until then we hadn't been involved in anything really nasty. From the first lineout the game degenerated into a big brawl. It was the first time in New Zealand that we had retaliated – to such an extent that, had there been yellow cards in those days, there would have been at least ten players in the bin. I had a bad day with the boot but a good game otherwise, finding the ball a little bit difficult. In New Zealand, they sometimes used to blow the ball up to make it very hard, which made kicking very difficult. Unless you spun it into a torpedo kick, the thing would shoot off anywhere. We were very pleased to come through such a tough game and win 12–6.

We next headed for Rotorua and a game against a combined Thames Valley and Bay of Plenty side. It was a most unusual place. It had hot springs but it was a very smelly place due to sulphur from a volcano which you could see in the distance. It was most unusual to see all this mud bubbling about everywhere and in the middle of the springs were geysers. If you put a block of soap down into the hole, you would get a huge ball of boiling hot foam coming up in a huge spray. They made good use of all this free hot water which was always available from these springs. One evening I was invited to try out a mud bath. I spent an hour laying there, enjoying the warmth, but when I came out I felt knackered. I didn't know what had happened to me but, the next day when I got up, I felt great, so it must have done something good.

I had been rested for this game, which we were supposed to win handsomely but we struggled a bit and scraped out a 26 points to 24 win in the end.

Our next game was against North Auckland in a place called Whangarei. We enjoyed a super day when we took a boat out and had a lovely time travelling from small island to small island and eating a picnic. The game itself was nowhere near as relaxing as the home team was one of the most powerful New Zealand teams of the lot and, in their captain, Peter Jones, they had an old adversary of northern hemisphere rugby. He was a giant of a man, about 6 feet 6 inches and 17 stone, who had been a huge success on a previous New Zealand tour of Great Britain.

I think they fancied their chances that day but unfortunately for them they found many of the Lions at their very best and we really took them to the cleaners, winning by 35 points to 13. Whangarei had the tallest goalposts I had ever seen in my life, 84 foot high and reported to be the tallest in the world. Apparently, the trees grew very tall there and all the sailing ships used to dock there if they'd lost a mast on their way around Australia and New Zealand. It was a great day for me because I couldn't miss those posts. I managed to kick four penalties and five conversions. I shall always remember the huge Peter Jones breaking downfield. I could see him coming towards me like a lumbering giant when our wing, Peter Jackson, came from nowhere and put in a blow behind the knees that felled him like a giant tree – the ground trembled in front of me as he fell.

Again, a report from the game was personally very flattering, but only served to make me wish I had been able to overcome my injury earlier in the tour. It read:

> The outstanding player on the field was fullback Terry Davies who scored 23 points for the visitors from his boot. His accuracy was such that he succeeded with nine attempts out of 12. All except one was acutely angled. Apart from his goal-kicking he inspired the Lions with the courage of his general play and repeatedly repelled strong attacking moves. His line-kicking was almost perfect, his positional play excellent and his tackling deadly.

I think we would have liked to have stayed in the Bay of Islands for a few days but the arrangements had been made and there was a reluctance to change them from the management point of view because we only had a week before the final Test in Auckland.

The fourth Test was the last chance for us to redeem

ourselves. Mr Scotland, our secretary, had decided to go fishing for four days and Alf Wilson, our manager, decided to go off with his wife just days before the game. We were on our own really, which is how it had been most of the tour. Undeterred, we did some light training and relaxed for the whole week – there was nothing strenuous about it as we were fit and there was no point in over-training.

It was coming into late spring and we had a thoroughly enjoyable few days. I must admit we didn't miss the management at all. We trained and we swam in the sea and it was lovely, it was great to relax during that week. A headline in one of the New Zealand papers said, 'What are the Lions doing?' They said we were not training properly or taking the game seriously.

The day before the Test Mr Wilson resurfaced and told me that I was playing. We set upon the tactics of hit and run and keeping the ball away from the New Zealand pack because the weather had been brilliant. Typically, when we woke on the Saturday morning it was tipping down with rain. All our plans had to be changed because it was now going to be a confrontational game and we had to take our opportunities as they came. Despite the conditions we did brilliantly, scoring three tries in the process and, when the final whistle went, we were all ecstatic as we had won by 9 points to 6; three tries against two penalties.

We had proved that we could beat the All Blacks and we did it with panache and great rugby. And it wasn't a fluke – we could, and perhaps, should have done it three times. After all, we had outscored them by nine tries to seven across the four Tests. In all 25 matches on the New Zealand leg of the tour, we scored a total of 582 points and only conceded around half that number, 266.

What really stands out when I look back at the last Test is that our Nemesis, Don Clarke, had a penalty kick in the last few minutes which could have denied us the win. The response to his miss from a huge New Zealand-dominated crowd is best summed up by a newspaper report:

> The roar which greeted the sight of the ball slewing away to one side of the posts could not have been more spontaneous if it had been inspired by a winning try. I can scarcely think that anyone left Eden Park feeling sorry that the Lions now had one Test victory to take home.

The headlines said it all:

Lions Bow Out in Blaze of Glory

and

Lions Show What Might Have Been

As we left the field after that final Test the crowd rose to its feet to sing 'Auld Lang Syne'. I'm sure they were of the same opinion as us, that it was a sad time. We were leaving New Zealand and it meant that they were going to miss a bit of excitement in their lives. And I for one, having got some form at the end of the tour, was reluctant to come home. I was ready to go on for another six months because I was playing well, had my fitness back and was raring to go.

As J B G Thomas wrote:

> 'The best fullback ever to visit New Zealand.' That was the title given to the fair-haired smiling Terry Davies of Llanelli here last night as a result of his magnificent displays on two successive Saturdays against North Auckland and in the Test won against New Zealand – two really hard matches. 'We wish we had him to take with us to South Africa next year,' said an All Black selector, and that is high praise, for Don Clarke, the 18 stone All Black fullback, has until now been regarded as the best in the world.

The next day we left Auckland early in the morning. It was a very sad day. We had had four glorious months in this brilliant country and I had thoroughly enjoyed it. I was more than pleased to be on such a great tour, such a trek all over New Zealand. I found the people a bit like the Welsh – very generous and welcoming.

When I think about what we accomplished, it is extraordinary. We went all the way to Australia and New Zealand without a recognised coach, with a squad made up of four different nationalities, yet played superbly together, winning the series in Australia 2–0 and really taking New Zealand to the cleaners at times. I think perhaps New Zealand were over coached and relied upon their forward monopoly but, having said that, we played such a swashbuckling style and had such great running players, we would have made any team look ponderous. No wonder the people of New Zealand wanted to come and see us play. I am quite sure that if you ask the people who saw us play at that particular time, our playing was a huge part in their lives as far as rugby is concerned. We gave them something totally different to how New Zealand were playing.

The articulate Cliff Morgan, a former team-mate of mine with Wales of course, wrote the foreword for Paul Verdon's excellent record of the 1959 tour, *Kings of Rugby*. Morgan, himself a Lion who had retired by the time of the New Zealand tour, wrote:

I have often wondered if the game of rugby football had ever known a team that announced all-round genius more eloquently than the 1959 Lions. This was a team that made the whole of New Zealand smile and enjoy the exciting, running rugby that displayed their natural way of playing and their competitive nature, which resulted in scintillating, exhilarating and glorious back play. Ronnie Dawson's team relished the true spirit of the game and this was equally matched by the All Blacks and the Wallabies, giving us a tour that is well worth marking before it completely disappears in the mists of time.

And the author adds:

I can understand the sensitivities of some of the All Blacks who played in the Test series. They beat the visitors in this hard fought series but ever afterwards, because of the way the series evolved, their achievement has been questioned... The Lions were an often spectacular team. Producing record scores in many provincial matches and outscoring the All Blacks in tries scored in the series.

He goes on to write about myself:

Although he did not find form for much of the tour, he ended it as one of the most highly acclaimed fullbacks to have toured New Zealand. The fair-haired, blue-eyed player, one of only two Welsh-speaking members of the Lions (RH Williams being the other), had an acute sense of position, an immaculate fielding and lengthy kicking game, and he could tackle like a demon.'

What pleased me most from the tour was that I had been selected, by the *New Zealand Rugby Almanac*, as one of the five best players during the whole time in New Zealand, alongside R H Williams, Ken Scotland and Bev Risman. There was only one New Zealand player included in the five, so I suppose that says something.

I was also pleased for my good friend R H who really was outstanding on the tour. The great Colin Meads was a youngster at the time and, while he was to go on to become one of the all-time greats of New Zealand rugby, my mate, R H, wiped the floor with him in the Test series. R H was such a brilliant second row, he was the strongest man I have ever seen playing rugby without going to the gym, it was all natural. He was 17 stone and 6 foot 3 and if there was a maul he would shake the whole pile of players to get that ball. Colin Meads went on to say he was the best second row he has ever played against.

I was also included ahead of the All Blacks' great Don Clarke in the team of the series by the *Wellington Evening Post*, despite just featuring in two of the four Tests. As I have said before, if my injury had been seen to earlier, then things may have changed because we missed an awful lot of kicks at goal. Even though injury restricted me to just 13 of the 31 games, I finished the tour as our leading points' scorer. In all, I kicked 21 conversions and 15 penalties.

We left New Zealand the day after the last Test and flew

to Fiji where we spent a relaxing day before going on to San Francisco, via Honolulu, and then on to play a couple of games in Canada.

In Canada our first game was in Vancouver against a British Columbia All Stars XV at the Empire Games Stadium. It was a really tight affair that saw us win 16–11 in very wet conditions. Having spent a number of days in an aeroplane really took it out of us, not to mention all the 'relaxing' since the last Test.

After the game we attended a reception at Vancouver University and on display there was the Welsh jersey I had given to those students after a game in Cardiff a few years ago.

Our next stop was Toronto for a fixture against East Canada which was a pretty easy game really as we strolled home winners by 70 points to 6. After the game we had a nice evening – there were quite a few British ex-pats living there – and the next day we flew home. When we arrived in London it was a bit like landing in Australia, as there were very few people there to greet us, just a bit of press and families. After all the excitement of New Zealand it was a bit of a letdown. We said our goodbyes to one another and off we went back to our own lives.

I arrived home on the Thursday and I played for Llanelli against Aberavon on the Saturday – just 48 hours after arriving home. The game was at Stradey Park and I had promised our captain, Onllwyn Brace, that I would play one game. I was glad that I did because I dropped two goals from the halfway line and got a standing ovation from the whole of the Llanelli crowd, which was magnificent.

One newspaper said the next day:

Making a triumphant return to Stradey Park, Wales fullback Terry Davies showed the 8,000 crowd the form which won him such acclaim in New Zealand. The band played 'For He's a Jolly Good Fellow' as Davies led his team out and responded by giving a display which will rank with the finest ever seen on this historic ground.

His performance had an electrifying effect on the rest of the Llanelli team. After a series of defeats, the Scarlets came into their own. Davies himself scored 13 of the points with a penalty, a couple of conversions, and two of the most remarkable drop goals seen on the ground. He began the scoring spree by dropping a goal from the touchline and just inside the Aberavon half and later, receiving almost on the halfway line in midfield, he shook off a couple of tackles and sent the ball soaring between the posts.

Chapter 15

Retirement

I WAS SOON brought back down to earth when I looked at my bank balance and realised that I needed to get into my working clothes and start up the business once more. Remember, I had to give it all up in order to go on tour and our allowance was pitiful. If anything, I came back virtually bankrupt. A lot of the players had understanding employers who kept paying their wages while they were away. Ray Prosser told me that the Pontypool club had been very good to his wife, dropping in every week with some money so she could survive without him. Llanelli, on the other hand, presented me and R H Williams with a wallet each before we set off. I opened it up thinking there would be some cash inside to help us with the trip, but it was empty. That's how stingy the club was back then. My father, God bless him, gave me £20, which he couldn't really afford, and that helped a great deal.

I only played a couple of games over the next few months leading up to Christmas, as I had to work really hard at getting the business going again. My training also petered off. In hindsight, I should have continued playing because I was extremely fit and in a rich vein of form following the tour. But, before I knew it, the 1960 Five Nations was upon us and I had gone to seed, as it were. Of course, having been a star in New Zealand I was selected by Wales, more on reputation than merit as it turned out.

The first game, at Twickenham against England, turned out to be really messy and we lost by 14 points to 6. The game marked the arrival of the English outside-half Richard Sharpe, who ran rings around our open-side flanker, Haydn Morgan, who had had such a good tour in New Zealand. I wasn't on form either, and never really got into the game. R H Williams, who was captain, was the same. The fallout saw all the Lions dropped for the next fixture and that prompted R H to retire from the game entirely. I was just a spectator for the rest of the season, which really hurt. I understood perfectly when Ray Gravell used to tell the WRU. 'Don't select me, because it hurts too much when you drop me.'

When you're first dropped by your country you want to hide for a week. You don't want to meet people who say, 'Oh, they shouldn't have dropped you.' There's a lot of nonsense said by family and friends who mean well, but can't see past you. They have the impression that the WRU should be shot for dropping you. However, sometimes, when you're in the comfort zone as an international and you are selected for every game, it does you good to be dropped. It does the ego good and it certainly makes you try a little bit harder the next time you are selected.

The only silver lining from not playing international rugby that season was that I was able to put a lot more effort into my business and, towards the end of the season, it was thriving again.

Then my injury jinx struck again. Towards the end of the season I had a bit of a disaster playing against Swansea. The ball had been kicked behind me and, as it was running into the dead-ball area, I dropped on it but one of the Swansea forwards landed on top of me. I dislocated my left shoulder, which was my good shoulder. Fortunately, Dr Gordon Rowley was in the crowd at that particular time and he came down to the dressing room and within two minutes he had the shoulder back in place. I faced another six weeks out of the game. I thought, 'Here we go again!' My biggest fear was that it would develop into a real problem, one like I had experienced with the right shoulder. I had no intention of going through that kind of operation ever again, so I began to really think hard about retiring. I was only 27, so I delayed the decision and, by the time the 1960/61 season arrived, my shoulder had strengthened sufficiently to say, 'Right, I'll have another go at it.'

My decision was also influenced by the prospect of facing the Springboks, who were due to tour, once again. I dusted myself down and prepared to face the Welsh trials, which were an annual event back then. There would be three in total but most of the current internationals would feign an injury for the first one because they wouldn't want to play all three. That year I made myself available from the start, as I was determined to get my place back.

When the team was announced, following the final trial, the Big Five paid me a huge compliment by naming me captain. I was thrilled because I had given so much to rugby in Wales, having gone through all the injuries and coming back from them, I felt it was recognition and reward for my service.

South Africa arrived, as always, with a huge and powerful side that had acquired the nickname 'the unsmiling giants'. After the training stint on the Friday before the game, we returned to the Angel Hotel and had the great pleasure of meeting the Hollywood star Richard Todd. The actor, who was also a bit of a war hero having taken part in the D-Day landings, had come down especially to see the game, and I was fascinated by how short he was. He was thrilled that he had seen some of the big South Africans and he marvelled at the fact that we would have to cope with their size.

The game was played on 3 December. It had been a very poor winter with a lot of rain. All the pitches were sodden, especially the old Arms Park where you'd be dragging your feet 'out of the glue' as we used to say. When we got up on the morning of the game, there was a howling gale blowing and a terrific amount of rain was coming down. By lunchtime I was quite sure they would have to cancel the game; there was no way we could play in these conditions, they were really the worst I had ever seen. (As a matter of fact that evening, after the game, the River Taff was so swollen it burst its banks and flooded the Arms Park.)

To our amazement we were told that the game was going ahead. Now the South Africans had nice tracksuits to keep them warm when they went out onto the field, so I approached the WRU and said, 'Look, it's going to be freezing going out like this, could we also have some tracksuits?' They debated the matter for a while and came back and said, 'Yes, you can have tracksuits to keep you warm, but we want them returned after the game.'

The Springboks had a far heavier pack than we did and, with the conditions being so bad, we were going to end up with a large number of scrums and lineouts. As captain I had to make a decision whether it would be better to play against this terrific wind in the first half or to play with it in the second half, when the pitch would be really cut up. Of course, I opted to play against the elements in the first half with the tactic that we should try to hold them to the lowest amount of points possible. This we did very well. We tackled well and we kept them at bay for the almost the entire first half but, unfortunately, they managed to get a penalty goal over. We were quite confident at this stage, as was most of the crowd who were soaking wet, especially the ones who weren't in the stand. I had never played in such conditions before and never did afterwards.

Come the second half the Springboks dominated us. They dominated the lineouts and they dominated the scrums, starving us of ball. However, we did manage to score a try when our second row squeezed over beneath a pile of bodies, but the referee said he couldn't give the try because he couldn't see the colour of the jersey. We were all the same colour as the Arms Park's red mud! I pointed out to the referee that he was facing towards the South African tryline and it wouldn't be one of the South Africans that would be trying to get over – but that didn't go down very well.

With just 15 minutes gone in the second half, the referee called the Springbok captain, Avril Malan, and I together to consult over whether the game should be abandoned. He said he couldn't differentiate between the colours of the jerseys, which made it impossible for him to continue. He asked me if I would make a decision. I looked at Malan, who must have been about eight inches taller than me, and I said, 'Ref, look at this crowd, they've come to see us play. If I call the game off now and we lose, they'll hang me from the nearest tree tomorrow.' So we continued with the game but, unfortunately, we couldn't do the business and we ended up losing by three points to nil.

There was the usual inquisition. Some asked whether I should I have played with the wind in the first half? I don't think so. That decision was the right one because I had a feeling, with their domination in the second half, when we were tiring, the whole thing would have been too much for us. If we had, I am certain we would have lost by more points than three.

I had a chance for revenge ten days later when they arrived at Stradey Park to play Llanelli. Once again the weather was atrocious, but nothing like that Saturday in Cardiff. Years later our former First Minister, Rhodri Morgan, who is a massive rugby fan, recalled the game in an article in the *Western Mail*. He was in college at the time and had travelled to see them play against Cardiff where one of the South African backs, a big tough African called François Du Toit Roux, had fiercely tackled the Cardiff fullback and broken his arm or shoulder. He had then travelled down to Swansea and saw the same thing happen to the Swansea fullback by the same gentleman. And, of course, he couldn't wait to come to Llanelli to see what would happen to the Llanelli fullback! Surely enough, three-quarters of the way through the game, the move came when the outside-half lobbed the ball over our defensive three-quarter line and it hung in the air. I knew that Roux was coming; I could see him in the corner of my eye. I thought, 'Fair enough.' I did what I used to do in New Zealand; I swivelled around quickly, after catching the ball, to shake him over my back. Unfortunately, he hit me fairly high up but I still managed to swivel him around. The next thing I saw, he was sliding down the other side of me and landing flat on his back, having damaged a disc. I managed to get the ball into touch about 40 yards away and ignored him completely.

Rhodri Morgan said in his article, 'Davies had put the South African terror in his place.' It was funny because during the post-match dinner I was sitting opposite Roux, who had a rather painful look about him. He never spoke to me but he never took his eyes off me. He must have thought, 'Who is this smiling gentleman sitting opposite, looking all in one piece?' His only consolation was they had won 21–0.

I almost made it a hat-trick of games against the Unsmiling Giants, having been selected for the Barbarians in the final game of the tour in Cardiff. Unfortunately, I had to cry off because, unsurprisingly given the weather of the previous few weeks, I had managed to catch the flu and wasn't feeling very well at all. The Barbarians won that day; it was South Africa's only defeat in 34 matches on tour.

The next Wales game was in the 1961 Five Nations against the old enemy, England, at home in Cardiff. I must have done alright against South Africa because I kept my place in the team and was captain once more. It was another rainy day on the Arms Park and I'm quite sure that 1960/61 was one of the worst winters on record. To play at the Arms Park in those days, with Cardiff playing there as well, was always difficult. The pitch was dreadful every time it rained; it was like glue and your studs had no grip in that mud.

We won a close game 6–3, thanks to two tries by my pal

Dewi Bebb, who had just about forgiven me for flattening him at St Helen's a few years earlier! At the final whistle it was a huge relief because, having lost my first game as captain, it was an opportunity to make amends. It was also special because we had beaten England! What I didn't know at the time was that game was to be the last time I played for my country at home.

Away from rugby my business was taking its toll. I was very busy and I was finding it increasingly difficult to find time to play, let alone train. Come the end of the week I was knackered by all the heavy work of my timber business, and then playing on the Saturday lost a bit of its *hwyl* and charm. You get to a certain age when you think, 'I've got to make a living.' That becomes more important than anything else.

I was also courting seriously at this time. I had met the girl of my dreams – Gillian, who 55 years later is still my wife – and we were hoping to get married the following year. I suppose I had lost a bit of the incentive to play that I had felt at a younger age. Although only 28, I had been knocked about a bit and it was time to make sure that nothing else went wrong in the latter stage of my career.

Our next game was up in Scotland and that was always a hairy place to go to. I had already tasted defeat up there on two occasions and it wasn't a happy prospect going up on a cold winter's day and running out onto that open Murrayfield with the huge bank overlooking you. When you start thinking like that you know that your heart isn't quite in it.

Scotland were always an awkward side. They tended to play the game at quite a pace with nobody really passing the ball about. They seemed to pile the pressure on all the teams that came to Murrayfield. And, of course, we would go with a huge crowd of supporters and their expectations were always enormous. You were always hopeful that you could win in Murrayfield but you went with some trepidation. It was always the most horrible place on a Sunday morning having lost, returning to the railway station and having to walk past thousands of Welsh supporters. And I faced that grim prospect for a third time as we lost that day, 3–0.

Thankfully, throughout my career, I never felt any disrespect from any Welsh supporter. That is something I am really pleased about.

The pressure of captaining your country is enormous and as a fullback the job is probably much more challenging than from any other position because you are too far away from play to make any real difference. A captain should really lead from the front. In my opinion, it is always best to have one of the forwards as captain. I found that I couldn't really get into the game. You are always thinking about what's coming next and having to cope with it. That kind of pressure didn't do me any good, I must admit. My hat goes off to people like Phil Bennett who took it as it came and did a wonderful job – it didn't detract from his playing ability at all. And then you had Gareth Edwards, who, while being probably the greatest player we have seen, was another who perhaps struggled a bit under the burden of captaincy.

As it happened, I was injured ahead of Ireland's visit to Cardiff and was unable to play in the game. Fortunately, I was able to take my place back in the team for the trip to Paris for the final fixture of the season, but I had lost the captaincy. It was my 21st appearance for Wales and to mark the occasion the French gave me a 21st-birthday gift which was a bottle of Cognac and six lovely glasses, which I've still got today. The gesture was particularly poignant because, although not made public at the time, I had made the decision that it was to be my last game for my country.

Paris in the spring was fitting for my last cap but it didn't turn out to be a fairy-tale end to my international career. France were developing into a fine team and we lost by 8 points to 6. There was the consolation, however, of seeing a fellow Bynea boy move a step closer to playing for Wales.

Kelvin Coslett had been brought over as reserve and we shared a room together in Paris. My brother Roy also came over and, as he didn't have anywhere to stay, he shared the room as well. We would sneak something up for him to eat and it was quite a pleasant trip altogether.

As a youngster I could see that Kelvin had potential, so I took him down to Stradey but he ended up playing for Aberavon. He used to practise kicking with me on our village field. I could see that he was having a problem with his style. He was a big lad and he was approaching the ball like a farmer, shaking from one side to the other. I said, 'You are off balance, you have to cool down. The thing to do is to have a little dance first, so you are balanced. When you feel that you are balanced, try kicking it.'

It worked and he adopted the style.

Kelvin took over from me as the Welsh fullback and had four caps before going North to play rugby league where he became quite an icon at St Helens and later a rugby league international playing for Wales and Great Britain. He is now deservedly in the St Helens' Hall of Fame. I like Kelvin very much; he's always got a huge smile on his face and no one deserved the accolades more than he did. I used to watch him on television and it used to make me chuckle when the great rugby league commentator Eddie Waring used to say, 'Watch how he prances before he kicks!'

On the subject of kicking for goal, I was basically self-taught. I used to practise a great deal. I used to go down to Bynea Rugby Club, even when I was playing for Wales, like Leigh Halfpenny does in Gorseinon. I used to dig a hole with my heel, set the ball down and aim it at the posts. If it was a short kick it would be upright; if it was a long kick and the wind was blowing, you would bend your body over the ball to keep it low; if the wind was behind, you would lift it high so the wind would take it. It all came naturally – nobody taught me how to kick. I used to take three steps back in a straight line and aimed my kicking foot, which was my right foot, with the tip of the ball and the posts. You did what all the golfers do and kept your head down and kept your eye on the tip of the ball.

I had no problems with taking the kicks. If it went astray you would correct it the next time. I find today's kickers, with all their various routines, very interesting. It's like an opera. Penalty kicks were still important in my time; I won a lot of games through kicking penalties.

However today I think the front row being penalised, the kickers, and the referees have now taken over the game.

I finished off the season with Llanelli before retiring from first-class rugby as well. News of my retirement was greeted with disappointment by the WRU and they did their best to persuade me to carry on. This led to an almost comical situation the following season when I decided that I would go back to my roots and help my village club out on the field of play.

We arrived to play against Brynaman in the west Wales league to discover that the Big Five had made their way up the Amman Valley in the hope of enticing me back into the international fold. I was reminded of this story many years later by great BBC Wales broadcaster Roy Noble, who lined up on the wing for the home side that day! What a game it was, as 29 players went hell for leather, doing their best to catch the eye of the selectors. I suppose they felt that if they played well enough they could be selected for the game against England at Twickenham!

As far as I am aware, I was the only player approached after the game but I refused to change my mind about retirement. In fact, I soon retired from the game altogether following a rather unpleasant local derby against Hendy. I had taken a high ball before being engulfed by the whole opposition pack, or so it seemed. Initially, I managed to keep on my feet but then I was dragged to the floor. I could hear one of the opposition shouting, 'He's down! Get him!'

That wasn't what I'd retired to my village side for, so I called it a day.

I had played for my country 21 times over a nine-year period and also represented the British and Irish Lions on two occasions – there was the knowledge that, without my catalogue of injuries, those totals could have been a lot more, but that is just the way life goes. I never dwelt on it.

There were never any regrets when I finished playing; my life was too busy for that. I got married and started building my own house overlooking the village where we still live today. And with plans to start a family it was time to earn some real money. I must admit there was plenty of hard work, with long days from 8am to 8pm, but from that hard work my business thrived. Just as in rugby, the same is true in business; you only get out of it what you put in.

CHAPTER 16

Life after Rugby

WHEN IT CAME to business, I basically taught myself. I didn't make many mistakes but when I did I learned from them and never made them again. I suppose I was a natural businessman, but I had to be. I had married and had three children to support, so it was a case of going to work each morning and saying. 'Right, how can I make some money today?'

I had a break when I secured a contract with Great Western Railway to dispose of sections of their lines that were being replaced. The farmers had been given grants from the Government at the time and I saw an opportunity to sell them the wooden sleepers and steel work. They sold like hotcakes and I soon realised that there was better business to be had in steel rather than wood.

I then looked at a group of companies in Bynea and Llanelli, namely Rees Industries Ltd, Rees Shipbreaking Co. and Lewis Foundry, which were all underperforming. They were running along similar lines to what I was doing with the railways; I was also buying the engines and breaking them up for scrap. I approached them: I think they were glad to see me because they were losing a lot of money at that time, and I bought them out for £40,000. I didn't have that kind of money so I had to persuade the bank to lend it to me. The bank reluctantly came up with the money and, within nine months, I had paid it back.

The business was underperforming but it had a good name and huge contracts. I saw that with the scrap business I could supply the foundry. Basically, I was recycling before anyone else. I was acquiring different metals and selling it on tenfold.

I also bought the scrap yard where me and my brothers used to play in the damaged aeroplanes during the war and the Vitraflex works in Dafen where I had worked as a 14 year old fresh out of school – not bad for someone who was once told by the Navy's doctors to get a light job brushing floors!

I sold up and retired in 1990, with the intention of living a quiet life but, when I looked at my village, I saw that it was in decay. Bynea has always had a special place in my heart, so I decided to do something about it and set up what became known as the Bynea Forum. The aim was to put something back into my community. I gathered some like-minded individuals around me, such as Councillor Gwyn Wooldridge, and we procured a lot of money in grants from the Government and Europe to improve the village. There's still a bit of work to do, but it's now a nice village again.

The other big project that caught my interest was securing the heritage of Llanelli Rugby Club in the wake of the decision to leave Stradey Park and move to the new Parc y Scarlets. I was absolutely against leaving Stradey Park behind – it was the heart and soul of the town – but you have to be realistic. I loved Stradey. I had played there alongside so many good friends, but you have to move with the times. That doesn't mean you should forget your past, though.

I was chairman of the Llanelli Former Players' Association at the time and I approached the region and asked what they were doing to keep the history alive? No one had an answer. I told them that I thought they should save the famous saucepan-topped goal posts and place them strategically in Llanelli. This has been accomplished and today you can find one set on the Berwick roundabout on the eastern gateway to the town, and the other was unveiled to the west, in Sandy Water Park, complete with a stainless steel artwork, by Llanelli artist Roger Lewis, of Phil Bennett sidestepping an All Black!

I also managed to help persuade Taylor Wimpey, which bought Stradey Park and replaced it with houses, to commemorate the heritage of the area. Today you will find several of the new streets named after Llanelli legends, and a memorial square with a display board and standing stone bearing the iconic image of Delme Thomas being hoisted shoulder high after that famous victory against the New Zealand.

Hopefully, it will serve to attract people to the town and allow them to make a pilgrimage, of sorts, to the spiritual home of Llanelli Rugby Football Club.

I suppose my efforts didn't go unnoticed as, in 2013, I had the opportunity to meet the Queen once more while being presented with an MBE for services to the communities of Bynea and Llanelli. I am extremely grateful to my good friend Doug Williams, brother of the fearless Ozzie Williams, for putting my name forward. It was nice to receive the honour but also good to be able to take my wife Gillian and children Matthew, Richard and Nicola with me to the Palace.

Prior to receiving our honours the recipients – there were several dozen of us – had to wait in this special room. I remember noticing Mr Bean (Rowan Atkinson) was there to collect his award, but he kept himself to himself.

When my turn came I approached the Queen and said, 'Ma'am, this is not the first time that we have met. I had the great pleasure of being at your Coronation. You were very beautiful.'

She said, 'Mr Davies, that was a very long time ago.' I replied, 'You are still beautiful to me.' And a smile erupted over her face.

Afterwards this large Colonel led me away and he demanded to know what I had said to make the Queen smile. I replied, 'I told her a little Welsh joke,' before making a sharp exit.

I was brought up as a first-language Welsh speaker, and our culture has always been important to me, so I was pleased to have been elected to the Gorsedd of Bards when the National Eisteddfod was held in Llanelli in 2000. I was joined by Clive Rowlands, Delme Thomas and Ray Gravell, who went on to revel in his role as holder of the sword of peace until his untimely death. The only problem was you had to wear these green robes, and when my wife saw me she said, 'My goodness. You look like your mother!'

Then, in 2008, I was inducted into the WRU's Hall of Fame which is a humbling tribute when you look at the players there with you.

As far as rugby is concerned, I don't go to a lot of games any more. I miss the 3 o'clock kick-offs on a Saturday. At my age it becomes a problem finding your way home after evening games. I much prefer to put my feet up and watch games on television – not that I'm enamoured by the modern game. I think rugby has evolved into a turgid affair. I wouldn't say that we were better players in my day but we played a different game. It was more exciting; to fill stadiums up you have to be exciting. We basically played heads up rugby. Today they are playing with their heads down.

We relied upon skill and individual brilliance. The skills are still available but, unfortunately, most of the skill is with smaller people and the game has become dominated by giants. When we lost to Australia in the World Cup, if we had put Mathew Morgan on when they were down to 13 men, we would have scored two tries. I know the game has changed but, in my day, it was the small people who you couldn't lay your hands on. There were a lot of Shane Williams-type players in every team. As kids you would go out on the village green and there would be 50 kids there, so you had to learn quickly to avoid everyone. That's what happened with players like Phil Bennett and Jonathan Davies; they were in a big group of boys and they had to evade them.

While Wales have had a far better record over the last decade or so than my generation enjoyed, I am worried about the future of the game, as the entertainment value is all but broke. What we need is another Carwyn James to come along and fix it.

I'm not so sure playing rugby for Wales is still the big dream of every little boy, or girl, these days, but I for one am glad that it was mine. Through pulling on the famous red jersey, a boy from Bynea grew into a confident young man, who travelled the world and made many friends along the way, collecting countless memories to reflect on, now the journey is nearly over. For that I remain forever grateful.

Terry Davies
International Record,
1953–61

W ales
Australia: 1958
England: 1953, 1957, 1958, 1959, 1960, 1961 (c)
France: 1953, 1957, 1958, 1959, 1961
Ireland: 1953, 1957, 1959
Scotland: 1953, 1957, 1958, 1959, 1961 (c)
South Africa: 1960 (c)
Total for Wales: 21 games, 6 conversions, and 10 penalties
Total points: 42

B ritish and Irish Lions
Australia and New Zealand: 1959
Second Test, Athletic Park, Wellington, lost 11–8
Fourth Test, Eden Park, Auckland, won 6–9
Total for Lions: played 15 games, 28 conversions, and 17 penalties
Total points: 107

B arbarians
Terry played 13 games for the famous invitation side, including tours to Canada and South Africa, scoring 57 points.

Other
Terry was part of a combined England & Wales side that played against Scotland & Ireland at Twickenham in October 1959.

Swansea RF C record
1950–4: 53 games

Llanelli RF C record
1955–61: 150 games